A QUICK COURSE IN

POWERPOINT® 4

For Windows

Computer training books for busy people

JOYCE COX

POLLY URBAN

PUBLISHED BY
Online Press Incorporated
14320 NE 21st Street, Suite 18
Bellevue, WA 98007
(206) 641-3434
(800) 854-3344

Publisher's Cataloging in Publication
(Prepared by Quality Books Inc.)

Cox, Joyce K.
   A quick course in PowerPoint for Windows / authors, Joyce Cox
and Polly Urban.
    p. cm.
    Includes index.
    ISBN 1-879399-33-4

    1. Computer graphics.   2. Microsoft PowerPoint for Windows.
I. Urban, Polly. II. Title. III. Title: PowerPoint for Windows.

   T385.C69 1994   006.6'869
                       QBI94-889
                             94-067427
                             CIP

Printed and bound in the United States of America

1 2 3 4 5 6 7 8 9 P O P O 3 2 1 0

Contents

The Basics:
Creating a Simple Presentation

We edited sample text provided by the AutoContent Wizard,
using Slide, Outline, and Slide Sorter views,
to create this presentation.
We then printed the presentation in black and white
to produce overhead transparencies.

Toward a Healthy Environment

Ted Lee

Redmond Business Environmental Action Team

Vision Statement

- By the year 2000, all Redmond companies will have evaluated their business practices and implemented any changes necessary to promote a healthy environment

Goals

- Increase business awareness
- Encourage win-win solutions
- Stop waste
- Reduce the nation's garbage bill

Rationale

- If we don't do it ourselves, government will do it for us

Today's Situation

- 56 members out of 432 businesses
- 10 new members a month
- 5 Business Ambassadors
- 2 Pinnacle Sponsors
  - » GlassWorks
  - » EarthWare

How Did We Get Here?

- Chartered as a chapter of USA BEAT in 1989
- Originally staffed by volunteers
- Offices rented and a full-time coordinator hired in 1992
- First annual Achievement Awards in 1993

Activities

- Publish On the BEAT newsletter and online forum
- Maintain resource center
- Conduct on-site analyses
- Support local recycling efforts
- Community outreach

Join Us!

- Grass-roots effort
- Successful track record
- Strength in numbers

If we conducted a survey of people who use computers as part of their jobs, we would probably find that most survey respondents work with one or two programs most of the time, with another couple of programs every so often, and with a few programs once in a blue moon. And of the respondents who have some kind of presentation program installed on their computers, most would put that program in the second or, more likely, the third category. Very few people develop presentations for a living, and for most people, developing presentations is not a big enough part of their jobs to warrant spending hours becoming an expert.

Fortunately, sophisticated presentation packages like Microsoft PowerPoint provide a lot of support for occasional users. If you are suddenly faced with the task of creating a presentation—for example, to persuade colleagues to get behind a new program—you can focus on the message of your presentation and leave the aesthetic details to PowerPoint. In fact, as you'll see in this chapter, PowerPoint can even help you structure the content of your presentation so that you can successfully get your message across.

Throughout this book, we focus on how to use PowerPoint to produce simple yet effective presentations, and for our examples, we show you how to create presentations for a business association. You will easily be able to adapt these examples to your particular needs. Because adequate planning and smooth delivery are essential if you want your presentations to have maximum impact, we weave these topics into the chapters where appropriate. By the time you have worked your way through this book, you'll know not only how to use PowerPoint but how to develop and deliver a presentation that accomplishes your goals.

We assume that you have already installed both Windows 3.1 and PowerPoint 4 for Windows on your computer. We also assume that you've worked with Windows before and that you know how to start programs, move windows, choose commands from menus, highlight text, and so on. If you are a new Windows user, we suggest you take a look at *A Quick*

Course in Windows 3.1, another book in the *Quick Course* series, which will help you quickly come up to speed.

To follow the instructions in this book, you must be using a mouse. You can perform many PowerPoint functions using the keyboard, but the menus and buttons are intuitive and easy to use, and in no time at all, pointing and clicking your way around PowerPoint for Windows will seem perfectly natural.

It's time to get started, so let's fire up Windows:

1. With the DOS prompt (C:\>) on your screen, type *win* and press Enter to start Windows.

2. Open the Microsoft Office group window, and double-click the Microsoft PowerPoint icon. (If you don't have a Microsoft Office group window, open other group windows until you locate an icon that looks like the one on the right.)

Microsoft
PowerPoint

3. The first time you start PowerPoint, you are invited to take a tour of the program. Click OK to see the Quick Preview, or click Cancel to skip it.

4. After taking the tour or clicking Cancel, you see the Tip of the Day, which draws your attention to a particular feature, trick, or shortcut. To see another tip, click the Next Tip button. When you have finished reading tips, click OK. PowerPoint then displays this dialog box:

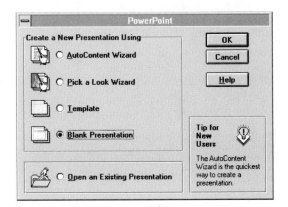

Tip of the Day

The Tip Of The Day dialog box will appear every time you start PowerPoint unless you deselect the Show Tips At Startup option before you close the dialog box. You can view the Tip of the Day at any time by choosing Tip Of The Day from the Help menu. If you then select the Show Tips At Startup option, the dialog box will once again appear every time you start the PowerPoint program.

As you can see, you can start a new presentation in one of four ways, or you can open an existing presentation.

Using the AutoContent Wizard

Suppose you are the coordinator for an organization called Redmond Business Environmental Action Team, or Redmond BEAT. (Readers who mastered Microsoft Word for Windows by working through *A Quick Course in Word for Windows* will recognize the name.) You have been invited to give a talk to the Chamber of Commerce of neighboring Kirkland, and you want to create a set of overhead transparencies that will not only explain what Redmond BEAT is about but also get people excited about your agenda. You are trying out PowerPoint for the first time, and you're cautious and want to take advantage of all the help you can get. For your first presentation, you're going to let the *AutoContent Wizard* be your guide. The AutoContent Wizard asks a few questions to get the ball rolling and then allows you to select one of six sample presentations as a starting point. Once you have selected a basic outline, you can fine-tune the presentation by adding, subtracting, or changing various elements to customize it. Follow these steps to use the AutoContent Wizard:

Basing the presentation on a sample outline

1. With the PowerPoint dialog box open on your screen, click the AutoContent Wizard option, and then click OK to display the first of four AutoContent Wizard dialog boxes:

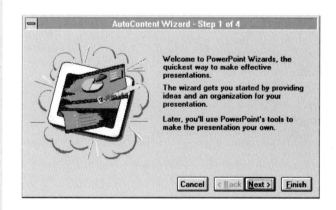

Wizards

Wizards are tools that are incorporated into several Microsoft applications to help you accomplish specific tasks. They work in the same basic way, regardless of the task or the application. They all consist of a series of dialog boxes that ask you to provide information or select from various options. You move from box to box by clicking the Next button, and you can move back to an earlier box by clicking the Back button. Clicking Cancel cancels the entire procedure.

2. Read the information in the dialog box, and then click Next to move to this dialog box:

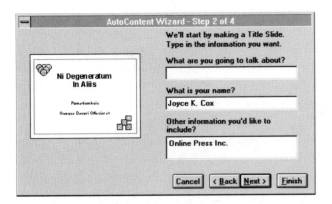

The information you enter in this dialog box will become the first slide, called the *title slide*, of your presentation. In the middle and bottom edit boxes, PowerPoint may have entered the name and company name used when the program was installed. The sample to the left gives you an idea of what the title slide will look like.

3. Type *Toward a Healthy Environment* in the top edit box, replace the name in the middle edit box with *Ted Lee*, and then replace the company name in the bottom edit box with *Redmond Business Environmental Action Team*. Click Next to display this third dialog box:

Entering the title slide text

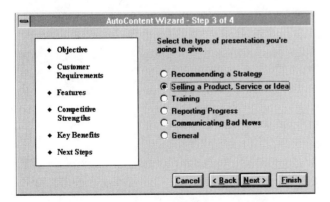

The titles of the slides in the selected presentation are shown on the left. You can click each option in turn to see which one most closely resembles the presentation you want to create.

4. Click the Recommending A Strategy option, and click Next to display the dialog box shown on the next page.

Selecting a type of presentation

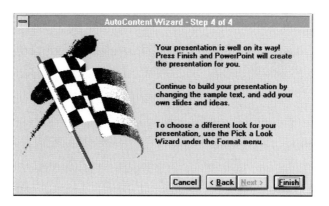

5. Read the information in the final AutoContent Wizard dialog box, and then click Finish. PowerPoint opens two new windows, and your screen now looks like this:

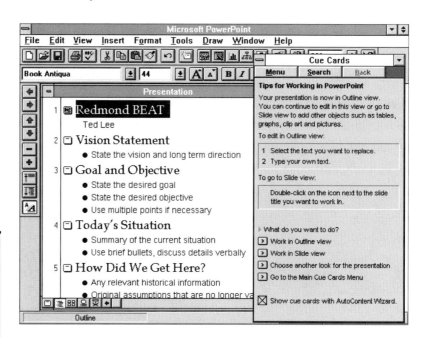

Cue Cards

You can display Cue Cards at any point while you are working with PowerPoint to get help with basic tasks and procedures. Just choose Cue Cards from the Help menu to display a window with a list of available topics, and click the topic you want. PowerPoint then displays step-by-step instructions. You can leave the window open while you work with your presentation. To close the window, double-click its Control menu icon.

6. The Cue Cards window on the right gives tips for working in PowerPoint. You can explore the Cue Cards feature later by choosing Cue Cards from the Help menu, but for now, give yourself more elbow room by double-clicking the Control menu icon at the left end of the Cue Cards title bar to close this window. Then click the Maximize button—the upward-pointing arrowhead—at the right end of the Presentation window's title bar to expand the window like this:

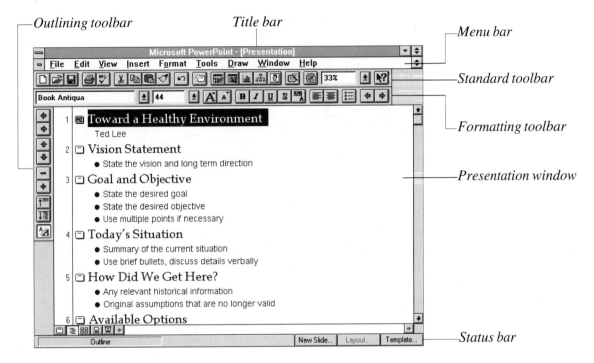

Outlining toolbar   *Title bar*   *Menu bar*

Standard toolbar

Formatting toolbar

Presentation window

Status bar

Like most Windows applications, the Microsoft PowerPoint window includes a title bar, a menu bar, toolbars, and a status bar. Let's pause to take a quick look at each of them.

The Microsoft PowerPoint *title bar* identifies the program. At its left end is the Control menu icon, which provides commands for manipulating the application and its window and for switching to other applications.

The *menu bar* changes to reflect the menus and commands available for the presentation component you are working with. To choose a command from a menu, first click the name of the menu in the menu bar. When the menu drops down, click the name of the command you want. To close a menu without choosing a command, click anywhere outside the menu or press the Esc key.

On the menus, some command names are displayed in "gray" letters, indicating that you can't choose those commands at this time, and some command names have an arrowhead next to them, indicating that choosing the command will display a *submenu*. You choose a submenu command the same way you choose a regular command.

The Office Manager toolbar

If Microsoft Office is installed on your computer and is started automatically when you start Windows, the Office Manager toolbar appears at the right end of the title bar (see the screen shown on page 123). The buttons on this toolbar enable you to quickly switch from one Office application to another without having to return to Program Manager.

Some command names are followed by an ellipsis (...), indicating that you must supply more information in a *dialog box* before PowerPoint can carry out the command. You sometimes give the necessary information by typing in an edit box. At other times, you might select options from list boxes or from groups of check boxes and option buttons. You'll use many types of dialog boxes as you progress through this book, and you'll see how easy they are to work with.

The *toolbars* are rows of buttons that quickly access the most commonly used menu commands. Currently, you see the Standard and Formatting toolbars across the top of the window and the Outlining toolbar down the left side. To avoid confusion, a feature called *ToolTips* helps you determine the functions of each button. When you point to a button, ToolTips displays a pop-up box with the button's name and provides a brief description of the button's function at the left end of the status bar.

ToolTips

The *status bar* at the bottom of your screen displays messages and gives helpful information. At its right end are three buttons that enable you to quickly create a new slide (see page 17), change a slides's layout (see the tip on page 17), or change the template that controls the overall look of the presentation (see page 39).

Taking up most of your screen is your new presentation, which PowerPoint displays in *Outline view* in the *Presentation window*. The first topic is the title-slide information you entered in the second AutoContent Wizard dialog box. The remaining topics are PowerPoint's suggestions as to the items you might want to cover when recommending a strategy. Each topic supplied by PowerPoint is designated by a number and a small slide icon to indicate that the topic will appear as the title of a slide. Subtopics are indented and bulleted to indicate that they will appear as bulleted items on their respective slides.

Saving the Presentation

Before we go any further, let's save the presentation. To save a new presentation, you click the Save button or choose Save

Shortcut menus

For efficiency, the commands you are likely to use with a particular element of a presentation, such as a bulleted list, or of the window, such as a toolbar, are grouped on special menus called *shortcut menus*. You can access an element's shortcut menu by pointing to that element and clicking the right mouse button. (This action is known as *right-clicking*.) In this book, we give instructions for choosing shortcut menu commands only when that is the most efficient way of accomplishing a task, but you might want to experiment with these menus to become familiar with them.

As from the File menu. PowerPoint displays a dialog box in which you specify the presentation's name. Thereafter, clicking the Save button or choosing the Save command saves the presentation without displaying the Save As dialog box because the presentation already has a name. Follow these steps:

1. Choose Save As from the File menu. PowerPoint displays the Save As dialog box:

Saving for the first time

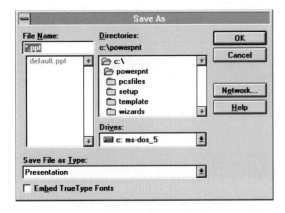

2. With *.ppt highlighted, type *redbeat1* in the File Name edit box. (You don't need to supply an extension; PowerPoint automatically uses PPT if you don't specify something else.)

3. Click OK. PowerPoint displays the Summary Info dialog box:

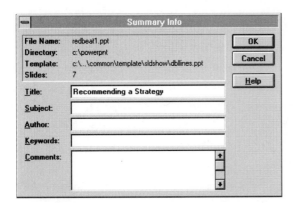

PowerPoint automatically displays the Summary Info dialog box the very first time you save a file. (You can display the dialog box at any time by choosing Summary Info from the File menu.) If you need to locate the REDBEAT1 presentation later, you can use the Find File command on the File menu to search for files on your hard drive based on the

Saving in a different directory

The file will be saved in the directory designated by the path above the Directories list. For example, the path C:\POWERPNT means that the file will be saved in the POWERPNT directory on your C drive. If you want to store the file in a different directory, you need to switch to the correct directory before you click OK to save the file. Double-click a directory icon in the Directories list to select that directory, display its files in the File Name list, and display its subdirectories in the Directories list. Double-click a subdirectory icon to display its files and subdirectories, and so on.

information you enter in this dialog box. (If you don't anticipate using this method of finding files, you can tell Power-
Point not to display this dialog box by choosing Options from
the Tools menu, clicking the Prompt For Summary Info
option to deselect it, and clicking OK.) For this example, we'll
enter only a title, subject, and author's name in the dialog box:

1. In the Title edit box, replace *Recommending a Strategy* with
   Redmond BEAT, and press Tab.

2. In the Subject edit box, type *Introduction*, and press Tab.

3. In the Author edit box, type *Ted Lee*, and then press Enter to
   close the dialog box. You return to your presentation, where
   REDBEAT1.PPT has replaced *Presentation* in the title bar.

From now on, you can simply click the Save button any time
you want to save changes to this presentation. Because Power-
Point knows the name of the presentation, it overwrites the
previous version with the new version. If you want to save
Saving a previous version   your changes but preserve the previous version, you can assign a different name to the new version by choosing the Save
As command from the File menu, entering the new name in
the File Name edit box, and clicking OK.

Switching to Slide View

Above the status bar in the bottom left corner of the Presentation window is a row of buttons that you use to switch from
one view of your presentation to another. Right now you are
in Outline view; notice that the Outline View button (second
from the left) is "pressed." This view allows you to see all the
topics and bulleted lists of your presentation in outline form.
You can enter and edit text in this view, but, as we discuss on
page 19, you'll probably use Outline view mainly for reordering the topics and bulleted text of your presentations. We
introduce you to the other views as you work your way
through the book, starting with *Slide view*, where you can
concentrate on the content of the presentation one slide at a
time. Follow these steps to switch to Slide view:

1. Click the Slide View button, or choose Slides from the View
   menu. Your screen now looks like this:

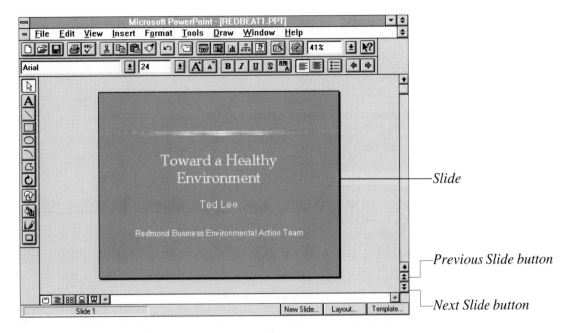

—*Slide*

—*Previous Slide button*

—*Next Slide button*

The Outlining toolbar has been replaced by the Drawing toolbar. Occupying the Presentation window is a representation of the title slide of your presentation displayed with PowerPoint's default *template*, which controls the appearance of the slide (see page 39 for more information about templates). The right scroll bar has acquired a Previous Slide button and a Next Slide button, which you can click to move backward and forward through the presentation's slides.

2. Click the Next Slide button to move to the second slide, which looks like this:

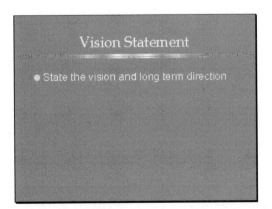

As you can see, the template controls the appearance of all the slides in the presentation, ensuring a consistent, professional look.

More about toolbars

By default, PowerPoint displays the toolbars it thinks you will use when working with your presentation in a particular view. You can display or hide any toolbar by choosing the Toolbars command from the View menu and selecting the toolbar's name. You can also select the toolbar's name from the shortcut menu displayed when you right-click any toolbar.

Before we customize this presentation, let's take a brief detour to discuss what makes a good presentation.

Presentation Do's and Don'ts

We've all sat through presentations that consisted of a single-page outline, copied onto acetate, and plonked onto an overhead projector. More likely than not, the speaker used a different piece of paper to block out the points he or she had yet to cover and moved this piece of paper manually down the page to indicate the current topic. Unless you have 20/20 vision and were sitting in the front row, you couldn't see a thing.

With programs like PowerPoint, presentations like these are, thankfully, a thing of the past. Nevertheless, it is easy to mar a presentation produced in PowerPoint with some of the bad characteristics of these old-style presentations. Here are some pointers for creating clear, concise slides:

Know your audience

- Put yourself in the shoes of your audience. Know as much as possible about them before you start creating your presentation and tailor its tone, words, and graphics appropriately.

Overall theme

- What points do you want your audience to remember one hour after your presentation? One week? Come up with an overall theme that you can reinforce throughout the presentation.

One idea per slide

- Make each slide responsible for conveying only one main idea that can be interpreted at a glance.

The fewer words the better

- Cut the verbage on each slide to the essentials. Never have more than six bulleted items on a slide. The more bulleted items you have, the fewer words you should use in each item.

Consistency counts

- Make sure your capitalization and punctuation is consistent and that your titles are constructed in similar ways. On any one slide, don't mix complete sentences and partial sentences.

The importance of good speaking skills

Above all, don't expect your slides to carry the entire weight of the presentation. When it comes right down to it, *you* are giving the presentation, not your visuals. To hold the attention of your audience—large or small—you must be poised and confident, and you must express your ideas clearly and persuasively. Many day-to-day business activities—introducing a new product to a customer, conducting a meeting, or negotiating a contract, for example—involve making presentations of one sort or another, with or without visual aids. The ability to speak in front of a group of people is a necessary business skill that is worth cultivating, even if you don't anticipate ever addressing a room full of people.

Working with Text in Slide View

With that bit of philosophy out of the way, we are ready to customize the text of the slides created by the AutoContent Wizard. You can work with text in both Outline view and Slide view. In a strong presentation, each slide must stand on its own as well as contribute to the overall message, so when you first start creating presentations, you will probably want to work in Slide view to see how each slide looks. Once you have a few presentations under your belt, you might find it quicker to work in Outline view and then switch to Slide view to see the results. In either case, you can go back and make changes at any time, so don't worry about getting stuck with something less than perfect. In fact, it's often best to leave the fine-tuning until the end of the development process; too much fussing can bog down even a short project.

First, let's edit the existing slides so that they tell the story of Redmond BEAT. Follow these steps:

1. Select the text to the right of the bullet. You can use any of the standard Windows selection techniques; for example, you can click an insertion point in front of the *S* of *State*, hold down the Shift key, and click after the *n* of *direction*. PowerPoint highlights the entire sentence, like this:

Selecting text

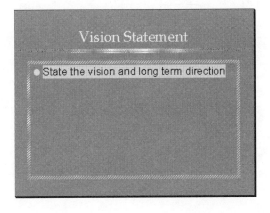

2. Type the following:

By the year 2000, all Redmond companies will have evaluated their business practices and implemented any changes necessary to promote a healthy environment.

3. Save your changes. (Remember to save at regular intervals as you work. A good rule of thumb is to save anything you don't want to do over again.)

Slide 2 looks pretty good, so let's move on:

1. Click the Next Slide button to display Slide 3.

2. Delete *and Objective* from the title; for example, you can click an insertion point after the *e* of *Objective* and press the Backspace key until only *Goal* remains.

3. Type *s* to turn *Goal* into *Goals*.

4. Click anywhere in the slide's bulleted list to activate it.

Selecting bulleted items → **5.** Click the bullet in front of *State the desired goal* to select the first bulleted item, and type *Increase business awareness* (without a period).

6. Repeat step 5 to replace the second bulleted item with *Encourage win-win solutions*.

Adding bulleted items → **7.** Repeat step 5 again to replace the third bulleted item with *Stop waste*, and then press Enter. PowerPoint moves the insertion point to a new line, preceded by a bullet.

8. Type *Reduce the nation's garbage bill*. Here are the results:

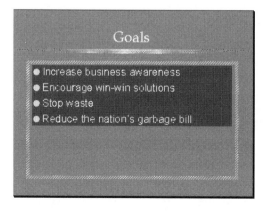

Adding Subordinate Points

Sometimes you will need to add subordinate points below a main bullet in order to adequately get your point across. Follow these steps:

1. Click the Next Slide button to move to Slide 4.

2. Change *Summary of the current situation* to *56 members out of 432 businesses*, and press Enter to create a new bullet.

3. Type *2 Pinnacle Sponsors*, and press Enter.

4. Click the Demote button on the Formatting toolbar. Power-Point replaces the bullet with a chevron and indents the line to show that this point is subordinate to the preceding bullet.

5. Type *EarthWare*, press Enter to create a new subordinate point, type *GlassWorks*, and press Enter again.

6. Now you want to stop adding subordinate points and create a new main bulleted item. Click the Promote button on the Formatting toolbar. PowerPoint replaces the chevron with a bullet and moves the line back out to the margin.

7. Type *10 new members a month*.

8. Finally, replace the *Use brief bullets* item with *5 Business Ambassadors*. Slide 4 now looks like this:

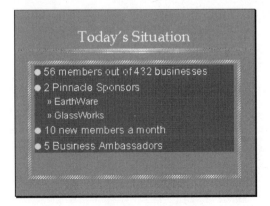

Deleting Bulleted Items

Customizing Slides 5, 6, and 7 involves making a few changes to the text supplied by the AutoContent Wizard and deleting one of the bulleted items. Follow the steps on the next page.

Five levels of bullets

PowerPoint allows you to create up to five levels of bulleted items on a slide, but we recommend that you use no more than two. Using more than two levels almost always results in crowded slides that are difficult to read and hard to understand.

1. Click the Next Slide button, replace the first bulleted item with *Chartered in 1989 as a chapter of USA BEAT*, replace the second bulleted item with *Originally staffed by volunteers*, and press Enter.

2. Add two more bulleted items so that Slide 5 looks like this:

3. Click the Next Slide button, and change the title and bulleted list of Slide 6 so that it looks like this:

The fewer bulleted items the better

The default slide template allows you to enter eight single-line bulleted items on a slide, but eight is really too many. As we said on page 12, you will stand a better chance of getting your point across to your audience if you limit the number of bulleted items to no more than six single lines. The more bullets you have on a slide, the harder it is for your audience to focus on any one of the points you are trying to make. If you have many bulleted items, try to find ways of breaking them up into logical groups and use a different slide for each group.

The last slide in the presentation has one more bulleted item than you need. Here's how to edit this slide:

1. Click the Next Slide button, and change the title to *Join Us!*

2. Change the first bulleted item to *Successful track record*, the second to *Strength in numbers*, and the third to *Grass-roots effort*.

3. Select the fourth bulleted item, press Backspace to delete the text, and press Backspace again to delete the bullet.

Adding Slides

You've reached the end of the presentation provided by the AutoContent Wizard. Suppose you want to add another slide. If you click the Next Slide button, PowerPoint simply beeps and displays the message *This is the last slide in the active presentation* in the status bar. Here's how to add the slide:

1. Click the New Slide button at the bottom of the Presentation window to display this dialog box:

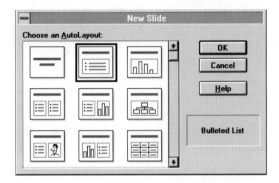

PowerPoint provides 20 predefined slide layouts, called *Auto-Layouts*, plus one "clean slate" that you can use to design a slide layout of your own. The nine most common Auto-Layouts are currently visible in the dialog box. The active slide's AutoLayout is selected, as indicated by the thick black border. The name of the selected AutoLayout appears in the box in the bottom right corner. You can scroll the other AutoLayouts into view by using the scroll bar to the right.

AutoLayouts

2. Click each of the visible AutoLayouts to learn its name.

3. When you are ready, select the Bulleted List AutoLayout, and click OK. PowerPoint displays this blank slide:

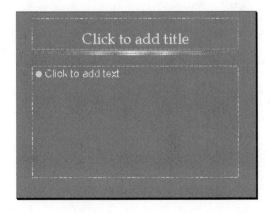

Changing a slide's layout

To change the layout of a slide, simply select the slide, and click the Layout button at the bottom on the Presentation window. The Slide Layout dialog box appears, displaying the same 20 Auto-Layouts that are available in the New Slide dialog box. Select the AutoLayout you want, and click the Reapply button.

Entering a new slide title

4. Click anywhere in the title area. The placeholder text disappears, and a blinking insertion point sits in the center of the area, waiting for you to type your own text.

5. Type *Rationale*.

Entering a bulleted item

6. Now click in the text object area below the title, and type *If we don't do it ourselves, government will do it for us*.

Fine-Tuning

You've completed the basic presentation. Now is a good time to move to the very beginning and scrutinize the slides one by one, using standard Windows editing techniques to make any necessary changes. Follow these steps:

Moving among slides

1. Point to the scroll box in the right scroll bar, hold down the left mouse button, and drag the box to the top of the scroll bar. As you drag, PowerPoint indicates which slide will be displayed if you release the mouse button at that point. Release the mouse button when *Slide 1* is displayed.

2. Press the PageDown key to move to the next slide, and continue pressing PageDown until you reach Slide 5, the first slide that needs editing.

Drag-and-drop editing

3. In the first bulleted item, drag across *in 1989* to select it. PowerPoint intuits that you want to select the entire date and the following space.

4. Point to the selection, hold down the left mouse button, and drag to the end of the bulleted item, releasing the mouse button when the shadow insertion point is to the right of the *T* in *BEAT*. PowerPoint moves the selection to the end of the line, adjusting the spaces appropriately. The three dates on this slide now all appear at the ends of their items.

Another couple of "niceties" will improve the look of this slide. Notice that the dates in the first and last bulleted items are sitting on lines all by themselves. You can make the slide seem more balanced by wrapping a little more text to the second line in each case. Try this:

Breaking lines aesthetically

1. In the first bulleted item, click an insertion point to the left of *in*, hold down the Shift key, and press Enter. PowerPoint inserts a "soft" return, breaking the line without creating a new bulleted item as it would if you pressed Enter by itself.

2. In the last bulleted item, repeat step 1 to insert a soft return to the left of *in*. Slide 5 now looks like this:

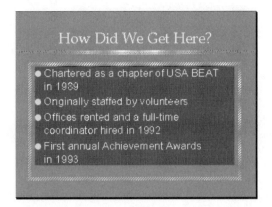

Reorganizing the Presentation in Outline View

Now let's move to Outline view to check the flow of your message from slide to slide. Organizing a presentation is often a trial-and-error process. You start by evaluating the major topics, add and delete a few subtopics, and then start moving items around and changing their levels until you are satisfied that your logic is tight and your argument persuasive. Because this process is an integral part of preparing a presentation, PowerPoint provides a special Outlining toolbar that puts the tools needed for organizing a presentation close at hand. Here's how to switch to Outline view:

1. Click the Outline View button in the bottom left corner of the Presentation window to see the presentation you developed in Slide view as a series of topics and subtopics.

2. Scroll through the presentation to evaluate its organization.

Reordering Text on a Slide

You can change the order of bulleted items on a slide by using cut-and-paste techniques in Slide view, but reordering items is even simpler using buttons on the Outlining toolbar. Try the steps on the next page.

1. Scroll the outline until you can see all the bulleted items under the *Today's Situation* topic.

2. Click the bullet to the left of *10 new members a month.*

3. Click the Move Up button on the Outlining toolbar until the selected item sits above *2 Pinnacle Sponsors.*

4. Now click the chevron bullet to the left of EarthWorks to select the item.

5. Click the Move Down button. *EarthWare* and *GlassWorks* effectively switch places.

Selecting a bulleted group

6. Click the bullet to the left of *2 Pinacle Sponsors.* PowerPoint selects not only the text adjacent to the bullet but also its two subordinate points.

7. Click the Move Down button once. PowerPoint moves the main bullet and its subordinate points to the bottom of the *Today's Situation* list, which now looks like this:

![Microsoft PowerPoint screenshot showing the outline view with Today's Situation topic and bulleted items]

Selecting parts of a slide

You can use many of the standard Windows text-selection techniques when editing text in both Slide and Outline views. For example, you can double-click a word to select it. In both views, you can click a bullet to select the bulleted item and its subordinate bullets. In Outline view, you can click the slide icon to the left of a topic to select the topic and all of its bulleted items. In Slide view, you can select an entire text object, such as a bulleted list, by clicking the object and then either choosing Select All from the Edit menu or pressing Ctrl+A.

Here's another way to rearrange bulleted items:

1. Scroll the outline until you can see the bulleted items under the *Join Us!* topic.

2. Click the bullet to the left of *Grass-roots effort*.

Reorganizing by dragging

3. Point to the selected text, hold down the left mouse button, drag the shadow insertion point until it sits to the left of the *S* in *Successful*, and then release the mouse button. PowerPoint moves the selection to its new location at the top of the bulleted list.

Reordering Slides

As you scroll through the outline of the presentation, you might notice a slide or two that would work better in a different location. However, if the outline is too long to fit on the screen all at one time, it is sometimes hard to decide on a precise order for the slides. This "can't see the forest for the trees" situation is easily remedied by *collapsing* the outline so that only the main topics are visible. You can then move a topic up or down in the outline to change the order of the slides in the presentation. Try this:

1. Click the Show Titles button on the Outlining toolbar, and then scroll to the beginning of the presentation. PowerPoint has hidden all the bulleted items and put a gray line under each topic to indicate the presence of hidden information, as shown here:

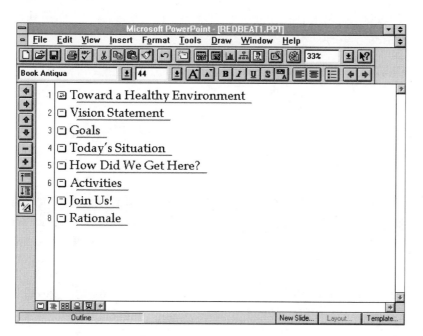

2. Click to the left of the number of the last slide (8) to select the slide and its hidden text, and then click the Move Up button until *Rationale* is the third topic in the outline.

3. Verify that the hidden text moved with the topic by clicking the Expand Selection button on the Outlining toolbar. Here's the result:

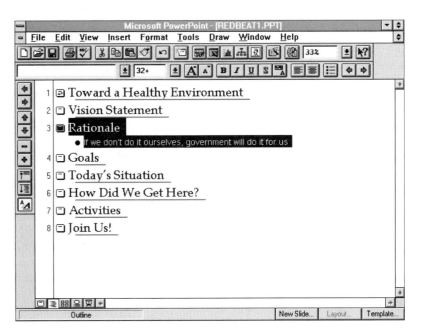

4. Click the Collapse Selection button to once again hide the bulleted item.

5. Click the Show All button to redisplay the entire outline in its new order.

Reordering Slides in Slide Sorter View

You've worked on individual slides in Slide view and on the presentation outline in Outline view. Now let's look at the slides from a different perspective. Slide Sorter view allows you to see your slides laid out visually. You can then add or delete slides or change their order. Here's how to rearrange slides in Slide Sorter view:

1. Click the Slide Sorter View button in the bottom left corner. When PowerPoint finishes redrawing your screen, it looks like this:

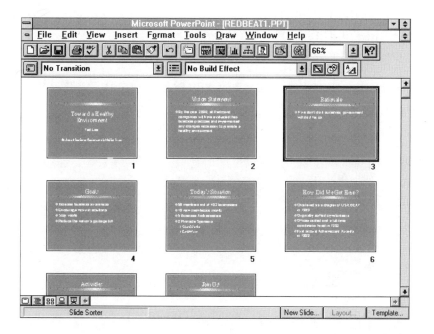

At the top of the screen, PowerPoint has replaced the Formatting toolbar with the Slide Sorter toolbar. Sketches, called *thumbnails*, of the presentation's eight slides are displayed with enough detail that you can get a good idea of how the slides look. Because the *Rationale* topic was selected in the outline, the *Rationale* slide is selected in Slide Sorter view, as indicated by the black border.

Thumbnails

2. Move the Rationale slide so that it follows the *Goals* slide, by pointing to Slide 3, holding down the left mouse button, dragging the shadow insertion point to the right of Slide 4, and releasing the mouse button. Slides 3 and 4 switch places.

Increasing or Decreasing the Screen Size of Slides

Although Slides 7 and 8 are only partially displayed, you can still work with the presentation in this view. But what if the presentation had 15 slides instead of 8? Fortunately, you can tell PowerPoint to make the slide thumbnails smaller so that it can show more slides on the screen at the same time. (At the smallest size—25% of full size—there is room for up to 28 slides.) When you work with small thumbnails, it's a good idea to also tell PowerPoint not to bother displaying your slides' formatting. Turn the page, and let's experiment.

The Slide Sorter toolbar

The buttons and boxes on the Slide Sorter toolbar enable you to add dynamic effects to an electronic slide show, such as fancy transitions from one slide to the next and slides that "build" themselves one bullet at a time. See Chapter 7 for information about how to create and work with electronic slide shows.

1. Click the Show Formatting button on the Slide Sorter toolbar to turn off formatting. Now the slides display only their topics in black type on a white background.

Zooming in and out

2. Click the down arrow to the right of the Zoom Control box on the Standard toolbar, and then click 33% in the drop-down list. Your screen now looks like this:

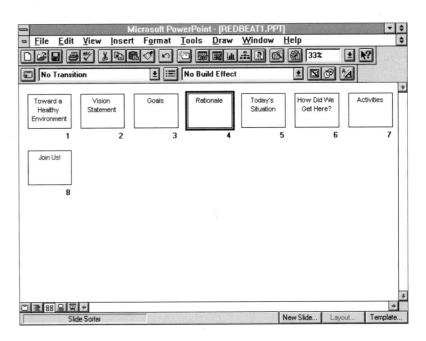

3. Click 33% in the Zoom Control box to highlight it, type *60*, and press Enter. PowerPoint redraws the thumbnails at the specified percentage.

4. Click the Show Formatting button again to turn formatting back on.

In Chapter 7, we talk about the other options available on the Slide Sorter toolbar. For now, let's see how to print the presentation you've created as black-and-white overheads.

Printing Black-and-White Overheads

In this chapter, we've worked with PowerPoint's default template to create a presentation destined to be printed on acetate with a black-and-white printer. In spite of all the advances in presentation technology, black-and-white overhead transparencies are still the medium of choice for the majority of people. Although the price of color printers is

Printer setup

If you have a choice of printers you can use to print your slides, such as a black and white printer and a color printer, you can select the printer for the current presentation by clicking the Printer button in the Print dialog box to display the Print Setup dialog box, highlighting the name of the appropriate printer, and clicking OK to return to the Print dialog box. If you want to change the printer that PowerPoint uses as the default, click the Select As Default Printer button before you click OK.

tumbling and the availability of display equipment such as
LCD projectors is more widespread (see page 139), the fact
is that most people don't want or need to purchase special
equipment for the rare occasion when they are called upon to
make a presentation. If making presentations is part of your
job or if your future career hinges on the impact of a particular
presentation, you will probably discount overheads in favor
of color slides (see Chapter 2) or an electronic presentation
(see Chapter 7). But be warned: No amount of color and
high-tech gadgetry can make up for a mediocre delivery style.
When all is said and done, it is what you say not what you
show your audience that will win them over.

As you'll learn in Chapter 2, PowerPoint has a whole library
of templates designed specifically for black-and-white overheads. However, you can get very good results with the default template used in this chapter, provided you know how
to tell PowerPoint to translate the on-screen colors into black
and white. Follow these steps:

Templates for black-and-white overheads

1. Turn on your printer, and load the paper tray with at least eight
sheets of acetate.

2. Choose Print from the File menu to display this dialog box:

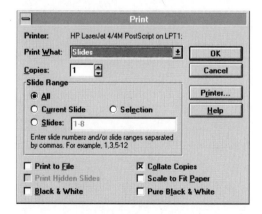

If you want to print the entire presentation with the default
settings in this dialog box, you can simply click the Print
button on the Standard toolbar. If you want to print only the
active slide or only specific slides, or if you want to change
any of the options at the bottom of the Print dialog box, you
must choose the Print command.

**Translating color to
black and white**

3. Click the Black & White option to tell PowerPoint to translate the colors in your slides to black, white, and shades of gray, and then click OK. PowerPoint then prints the set of overheads shown at the beginning of the chapter.

Getting Help

This tour of PowerPoint has covered a lot of ground in just a few pages, and you might be wondering how you will manage to retain it all. Don't worry. If you forget how to carry out a particular task, help is never far away. For example, let's see how you would remind yourself of the steps for saving a new presentation:

1. Click the Help button on the Standard toolbar. The pointer becomes an arrow with a question mark attached to it.

2. Move the Help pointer to File on the menu bar, and click to drop down the menu.

3. Click Save As to display a Help window containing information about the Save As command, and click the Help window's Maximize button so that your screen looks like this:

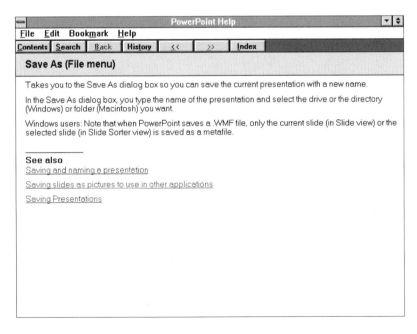

Getting help with dialog box options

Every PowerPoint dialog box has a Help button you can click to go directly to a Help window containing information about the edit boxes, options, and buttons available in that dialog box. You don't have to use the Help menu to access this information.

(Clicking a topic with a solid underscore in the See Also section takes you to that topic.)

4. Click the Contents button below the menu bar to display the main topics of information available for PowerPoint.

5. Click the Index button to display an alphabetical list of topics. The letters at the top of the screen provide a quick way of moving through the index.

6. Click the Search button to display this dialog box:

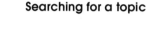

Searching for a topic

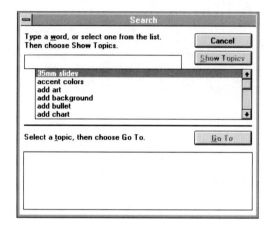

7. Enter the topic you're looking for; in this case, type *print*. PowerPoint scrolls its list of major topics to *print*. Click Show Topics to display a list of subtopics, select one, and click Go To to display the requested information.

8. Explore the other aspects of PowerPoint's Help system, and then click the Back button to retrace your steps.

9. When you're ready, choose Exit from the File menu to close the Help window and return to your presentation.

Quitting PowerPoint

You have seen how to use PowerPoint to create a simple text-based presentation. Easy wasn't it? All that's left is to show you how to end a PowerPoint session. Follow these two steps:

1. Choose Exit from the File menu.

2. When PowerPoint asks if you want to save the changes you have made to the open presentation, click Yes.

Printing a help topic

If you find yourself referring to a particular Help topic frequently, you can print the topic so that you have it available for future reference. Simply choose the Print Topic command from the Help system's File menu.

Presentation Makeovers: Getting Your Message Across

We used the Pick A Look Wizard to select a design
for 35mm slides and then entered the presentation's text.
We added formatting to individual slides
and changed the template by modifying the Slide Master.

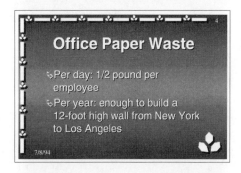

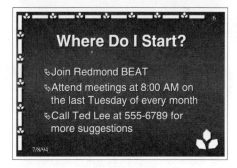

When you create a presentation in PowerPoint, you can exercise as much control or as little control as you want. In Chapter 1, you learned about the AutoContent Wizard, which provides you with both the design and content of your presentation. In this chapter, we'll introduce you to the Pick A Look Wizard, which helps you select a design template for your presentation but leaves the content up to you. We'll also show you how to format the text of your presentation and how to change the presentation's look and feel by simply switching to a different design template. We'll give you some pointers about changing the default background, fonts, and color scheme of your presentation slides, and then we'll discuss the mechanics of preparing a file to send to a slide production house.

Using the Pick A Look Wizard

As with the AutoContent Wizard, when you use the Pick A Look Wizard to create a presentation, you must be prepared to make some decisions and answer a few questions. For example, you have to decide right off the bat what type of output you want to create, such as overhead transparencies or 35mm slides. You also have to bear in mind the content of your presentation so that you can select a suitable design. For this example, you want to create 35mm slides for a presentation that will persuade local businesses to institute recycling programs and join Redmond BEAT in their efforts to promote recycling in the business community. It looks like you have your work cut out for you, so let's get moving:

1. If necessary, start PowerPoint by double-clicking the Microsoft PowerPoint icon in Windows Program Manager.

Accessing the Wizard

2. When the PowerPoint dialog box appears, select the Pick A Look Wizard option, and click OK. PowerPoint presents you with the first of nine dialog boxes. Take a moment to peruse the dialog box's contents, and then click the Next button.

Setting up for 35mm slides

3. In the wizard's second dialog box, select 35mm Slides as your output option, and click Next. (If necessary, you can change the type of output later; see page 140.)

4. In the third dialog box, which offers several design template options, click the More button to display this dialog box:

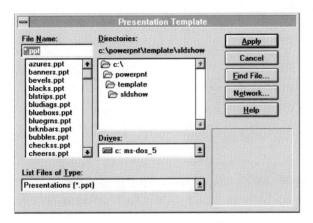

All of PowerPoint's built-in templates can be accessed via the Presentation Template dialog box. They are stored in three directories: BWOVRHD, CLROVRHD, and SLDSHOW.

5. To see all three directories, double-click the TEMPLATE directory in the Directories list. As their names suggest, these directories contain templates that can be used to create three specific types of output: black and white overheads, color overheads, and slides for a slide show.

Selecting a template

6. Double-click the SLDSHOW directory in the Directories list to display the names of the templates that PowerPoint's designers have created for slide shows.

7. Click any template name in the File Name list. A sample of the template appears in the bottom right corner of the Presentation Template dialog box. You can then use the Up and Down Arrow keys to scroll through the template files in the list, noticing the different effects created by each template.

8. When you're finished exploring, select the FORESTS.PPT template, and then click the Apply button. PowerPoint returns you to the wizard's Step 3 dialog box, with a sample of the FORESTS.PPT template displayed on the right.

Applying the template

9. Click the Next button to display the fourth Pick A Look Wizard dialog box, which allows you to generate additional types of output, such as speaker's notes (see page 152), audience handouts (see the tip on page 153), and outline pages.

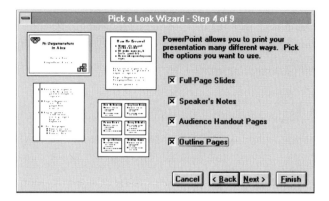

10. To create slides only, deselect the three options below the Full-Page Slides option, and then click Next to display the fifth dialog box.

11. Select the Name option, and enter *Redmond BEAT* in the accompanying edit box. Then click Next. (We'll add the date and page numbers later in the chapter.)

12. Because you deselected three of the four options in the fourth dialog box, the Pick A Look Wizard conveniently skips over the next three dialog boxes to bring you to the final dialog box. Click Finish to display the template in Slide view, like this:

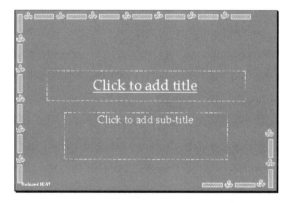

The Template option

You can bypass the Pick A Look Wizard's dialog boxes and go straight to the Presentation Template dialog box by selecting the Template option in the initial PowerPoint dialog box. After you select a template, PowerPoint displays the New Slide dialog box so that you can select a layout for your first slide. You can then create your presentation by adding text, charts, graphics, additional slides, and so on in the usual way.

Working with the Presentation Text

Having used the Pick A Look Wizard to select a design, you can turn your attention to the presentation's contents. Right now, you need to enter a little text on the title slide and then add some new slides to the presentation. Then we'll show you some ways of editing and formatting text.

1. Before you do anything else, click the Save button on the Standard toolbar, and save the presentation with the name *recycle*. (Remember, PowerPoint automatically appends the PPT extension to the filename.)

2. In the Summary Info dialog box, type *Recycling* in the Title edit box, then type *General Business Presentation* in the Subject edit box, and click OK.

3. Click the title area, and type *Waste Not, Want Not*.

4. Click the subtitle area, and type *Recycling Is Good Business*.

5. Now click the New Slide button at the bottom of the Presentation window to add a new slide to the presentation.

6. When the New Slide dialog box appears, select the Bulleted Text AutoLayout (the second AutoLayout in the first row), and click OK.

Now you're ready to add some astounding recycling facts and figures to jar your audience into action:

1. With Slide 2 displayed on your screen, click the title area, and type *The Cost of Waste in the U.S.*

2. Click the area below the title, and type *Today: $10 billion* as the first bulleted item.

3. Press Enter to start another bulleted item, and then type *By the year 2000: $100 billion*. (By the way, the source for these statistics is *The Recycler's Handbook*, published by Earth Works Press in Berkeley, California.)

4. Add a new bulleted list slide, and type *How Much Waste?* as the title, *Residences: 850 million tons* as the first bulleted item, *Industry: 6.5 billion tons* as the second bulleted item, and *Offices: 1/2 pound per day per employee* as the third bulleted item.

5. Save RECYCLE.PPT.

Cutting and Pasting Text Between Slides

If you take a look at Slide 3, you'll notice that the third bulleted item doesn't really fit. Follow these steps to add another slide and then do a little cutting and pasting:

1. With Slide 3 still on your screen, click the New Slide button, and add a new slide with the Bulleted Text AutoLayout.

2. Click the Previous Slide button to return to Slide 3, and click anywhere in the bulleted text to select all the bulleted items, collectively called the "text object."

3. Position the mouse pointer over the second bullet (the actual dot), and when the pointer changes to a four-headed arrow, click the mouse button once to select the second bulleted item.

4. Click the Cut button on the Standard toolbar or choose the Cut command from the Edit menu. The text is removed from the slide and stored temporarily on the Windows Clipboard.

5. Move to Slide 4, click the text object area, and then click the Paste button on the Standard toolbar or choose the Paste command from the Edit menu to paste the bulleted text onto Slide 4.

6. Edit the text to read *Per day: 1/2 pound per employee*. Then add another bulleted item, and type *Per year: enough to build a 12-foot high wall from New York to Los Angeles*.

7. Click the title area, and type *Office Paper Waste*. Slide 4 now looks like this:

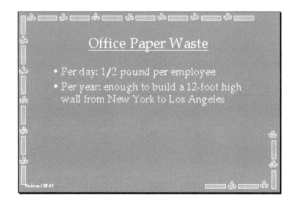

Now remove the extra bullet from Slide 3:

1. Move to Slide 3, click an insertion point just after the third bullet, and press the Backspace key.

2. Save the RECYCLE.PPT presentation.

Formatting Text

You have selected a design template to give your presentation a particular look, but keep in mind that you can still use text formatting to create special effects. For example, you can use bold and a larger font size to draw attention to major points and italic and a smaller font size to de-emphasize minor points. You can also select a specific typeface to reinforce the message you are sending to your audience. Sans serif fonts, such as Helvetica and Arial, have clean, crisp lines and lend themselves to presentations where the topics are short and to-the-point. Serif fonts, such as Times New Roman and Book Antiqua, have more detail and work well in presentations where the topics are longer. Bear in mind, though, that your company might require you to use a standardized set of fonts, in which case, you don't want to stray from that set (see the tip on page 40).

Which fonts to use when

Let's change some of the text formatting in RECYCLE. PPT using both the Formatting toolbar and the Font command. Follow these steps:

1. Display Slide 1 on your screen, click the title area, and then press the F2 key twice to select the title text.

2. Now take a look at the Formatting toolbar to determine which types of formatting have been applied to the current selection. The Font box at the left end of the toolbar displays *Book Antiqua*, which is the current font, and the Underline and Text Shadow buttons appear "pressed," indicating that the current selection is underlined and has a shadow.

3. Click the arrow to the right of the Font box on the Formatting toolbar to display a drop-down list of fonts like the one shown on the next page.

Serif vs. sans serif

The word *serif* means *stroke* or *line*, and the word *sans* means *without*. So serif fonts are those with strokes, whereas sans serif fonts are those without strokes. A good example of a serif font is Blackletter, which has delicate strokes trailing off the ends of the characters, especially the capital *B*. Century Gothic, on the other hand, is a sans serif font and doesn't have the extra detail of a serif font. A third category in the world of fonts is *script* fonts, which look as though they are handwritten. An example of a script font is ShelleyVolante.

4. Scroll the list, and select Arial.

5. Next, click the arrow to the right of the Font Size box on the Formatting toolbar to display this drop-down list of sizes:

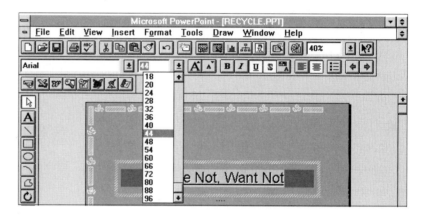

6. Select 60.

7. Finally, click the Bold button on the Formatting toolbar to make the text bold, and click the Underline button to remove underlining.

8. Now select the second line on Slide 1, *Recycling Is Good Business*, and choose the Font command from the Format menu to display this dialog box:

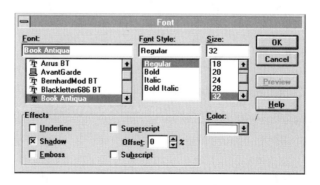

As you can see, the Font dialog box is useful because you can make a number of formatting changes all in one place. However, unlike changes you make with the buttons on the Formatting toolbar, you cannot see the effect of changes you make in the Font dialog box until you close it.

9. In the Font list on the left side of the dialog box, select Arial. Then select Bold from the Font Style list and 44 from the Size list. Click OK to implement your selections.

10. Click anywhere on the slide to deselect the text. Here are the results:

Repositioning and Resizing Text Objects

Before moving on to the next section, let's take a look at a couple of techniques you can use to resize and reposition the text objects on a slide:

1. Choose the Ruler command from the View menu to display PowerPoint's vertical and horizontal rulers. These rulers will serve as guides as you reposition objects on a slide.

2. Click anywhere in the title area. Then point to the frame surrounding the area, and click once or press F2 to select the frame. (You can also choose the Edit Object command from the Edit menu to select the frame.) Small squares, called *handles*, appear at the corners and along the sides of the object's frame, as shown on the next page.

Don't go overboard

When you select a font or fonts for your presentation, you should keep a few simple rules in mind:

- Use one font per slide.
- Use only one or two font styles, such as bold or italic, per slide.
- Watch out for certain style combinations. For example, text that is both italic and outlined is very difficult to read on a monitor or overhead projector.
- Try to use sans serif fonts wherever possible. They are easier to read on slides and overhead transparencies than serif fonts.
- Steer clear of overused fonts such as Times and Helvetica. Try fonts with a little more pizzazz to keep your audience interested. (Don't get carried away though. You want your fonts to be legible.)
- If you're having slides or overhead transparencies made, be sure your service bureau can produce the same fonts.

You can drag the handles to resize the object's width and/or height. To resize the object's width and height proportionally, drag one of its corner handles.

Text wrapping

If you resize a text object, the text inside the object will wrap to fit the object's new size. For example, a single line of text in an object might wrap to two lines when you decrease the object's size. You can control whether text wraps or not by first selecting the text object and choosing Text Anchor from the Format menu. Then, when the Text Anchor dialog box appears, deselect or select the Word-Wrap Text In Object option, and click OK. When you turn text wrapping off by deselecting this option, any text that does not fit within the object's frame continues beyond the frame's borders and, if necessary, even beyond the edges of the slide.

3. Move the title up by pointing to the top of the frame (not one of the handles), holding down the left mouse button, and dragging up until the marker in the vertical ruler is at the 1 3/4-inch position. Dashed boxes move with the pointer to indicate where the title area will appear when you release the mouse button.

4. Next, click the text object area to select it. Then point to the frame surrounding the area, and click once or press F2 to select the frame.

5. Move the area to the right by pointing to the left side of the frame, holding down the left mouse button, and dragging to the right until the marker in the horizontal ruler is at the 2 3/4-inch position.

6. Now make the area narrower by first pointing to the right center handle. When the pointer changes to a two-headed arrow, hold down the left mouse button, and drag to the left until the marker in the horizontal ruler is at the 2 3/4-inch position.

7. Click anywhere on the slide to deselect the frame, choose Ruler from the View menu to turn off the rulers, and then save RECYCLE.PPT. Slide 1 now look like this:

Working with Templates

As we mentioned at the beginning of the chapter, the appearance of your presentation is controlled by the template you selected, and you can change the entire look and feel of your presentation by simply switching to another template. As you saw in the Presentation Template dialog box (see page 31), PowerPoint offers a wide variety of design templates to choose from, but you're not limited to these designs. In this section, we'll show you how to create a custom template for the times when the built-in templates don't meet your needs.

One bit of advice regarding templates: Because the design of the template is a vital aspect of your presentation, with the power to convey a positive or negative message based solely on its background and color scheme, you must always consider the effect any design will have on an audience when you create a presentation.

The effect of design on an audience

With that out of the way, follow the steps below to see how easy it is to switch from one template to another:

1. With RECYCLE.PPT displayed on your screen, click the Slide Sorter View button at the bottom of the Presentation window so that you can see all your slides at once.

2. Click the Template button at the bottom of the window to display the Presentation Template dialog box.

3. Double-click the SLDSHOW directory, if necessary, and scroll down to the FIESTAS.PPT file.

4. Double-click FIESTAS.PPT to apply it to your presentation, which now looks like this:

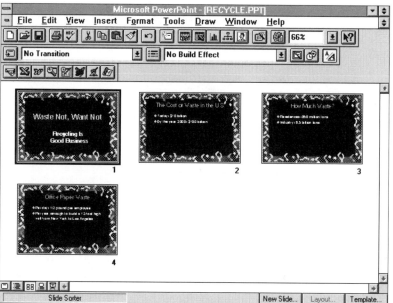

Hmmm, the party atmosphere definitely doesn't fit the mood of the recycling presentation. Let's stick with FORESTS.PPT as our template.

1. Choose the Presentation Template command from the Format menu.

2. When the Presentation Template dialog box appears, scroll down to FORESTS.PPT, and double-click it.

Creating a Custom Template

You can manipulate the components of a template in a variety of ways to come up with a custom design. For example, you can add a company logo to the background or change the template's default font. You can also rearrange the objects on a template or add the date, time, and page (slide) number. PowerPoint even provides a dialog box in which you can create your own color scheme. In this section, we'll introduce you to some of the ways you can change an existing template to give it a personal touch. Before you get started, however, take a moment to add two more slides to the RECYCLE.PPT presentation:

1. Double-click Slide 4 to simultaneously activate the slide and switch to Slide view.

2. Click the New Slide button at the bottom of the Presentation window, and when the New Slide dialog box appears, select the Bulleted List AutoLayout, and click OK.

3. Click the title area of the new slide, and type *What Can I Do?*

4. In the object area, type the following, pressing Enter to start each new bulleted item:
   - *Start a recycling program*
   - *Educate employees*
   - *Buy post-consumer products*

5. Repeat step 2 to add another Bulleted List slide.

6. When the slide appears, type *Where Do I Start?* in the title area, and then type the following in the object area:
   - *Join Redmond BEAT*
   - *Attend meetings at 8:00 AM on the last Tuesday of every month*
   - *Call Ted Lee at 555-6789 for more suggestions*

Changing the Background and Font

You can change a template's background and font via the Slide Master. As its name suggests, the Slide Master controls a number of elements on the slides, such as the graphic objects on the background and the fonts used in the titles and text. When you make a change to the Slide Master, all the slides in your presentation are affected. Follow these steps to create a custom template:

The Slide Master

1. Choose the Close command from the File menu to close RECYCLE.PPT. If PowerPoint asks whether you want to save your changes, click Yes.

Closing the presentation

2. With a blank Presentation window on your screen, click the New button on the Standard toolbar to display this dialog box:

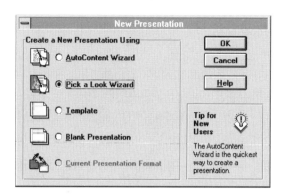

The New Presentation dialog box is similar to the PowerPoint dialog box, with the exception of the last option, Current Presentation Format, which allows you to create a new presentation based on the formatting of the current presentation. (This option is not available unless a presentation is open.)

3. Select the Template option, click OK to display the Presentation Template dialog box, and double-click FORESTS.PPT.

4. In the New Slide dialog box, accept the default AutoLayout by clicking OK. (The particular AutoLayout is incidental for our purposes.)

Displaying the Slide Master

5. When the new slide appears on your screen, choose Master and then Slide Master from the View menu to display this Slide Master:

Saving a new template

6. Click the Save button on the Standard toolbar, and when the Save As dialog box appears, double-click the TEMPLATE directory. Then double-click the SLDSHOW directory, and save the file with the name *trees*.

Now you're ready to begin modifying the new TREES.PPT template:

1. Click anywhere in the decorative "tree" border to select it, and then choose the Ungroup command from the Draw menu. As shown here, PowerPoint surrounds each object with handles so that you can work with the individual objects:

"Ungrouping" a graphic

2. To remove the handles, click the Selection Tool button at the top of the Drawing toolbar on the left side of the Presentation window.

3. Now for the tricky part. Position the mouse pointer (aka the *selection tool*) in the bottom right corner of the Slide Master, just inside the black frame. Hold down the left mouse button, drag to the left and up to draw a selection box around the entire border in that corner, and release the mouse button. You know the border is selected when PowerPoint surrounds it with handles, like this:

Selecting multiple graphic objects

4. Now press the Delete key to delete the corner border.

Selecting a single graphic → 5. Click the "triple leaves" graphic in the bottom left corner of the border to select it, like this:

Copying a graphic → 6. Now copy the graphic to the bottom right corner of the Slide Master. Point to the selected graphic, and simultaneously hold down the Ctrl key and the left mouse button. (A small plus sign next to the mouse pointer indicates that you are copying rather than moving the selected graphic.) Drag the graphic across the Slide Master, releasing the Ctrl key and mouse button to drop the graphic into place.

Sizing a graphic → 7. With the leaves graphic still selected, point to one of the top handles, hold down the left mouse button, and drag upward until the graphic is about 1 inch tall. Use the other handles to adjust the graphic's proportions until it looks like this:

8. Save TREES.PPT.

You'll recall that earlier in the chapter you changed the title and subtitle fonts on Slide 1 of RECYCLE.PPT to the sans serif font Arial. In addition to changing the font on individual slides, you can change the font on the Slide Master to change the font for the entire presentation. Follow these steps to change the default font:

1. Click the title area on the Slide Master, and choose Font from the Format menu to display the Font dialog box.

Changing the Slide Master font and font size

2. Select Arial in the Font list, Bold in the Font Style list, and 60 in the Size list.

3. Deselect the Underline option in the Effects section, and then click OK.

4. Now click the text object area on the Slide Master, and then select the text of the first bulleted item. (You're only interested in the first bulleted item because the slides in this presentation contain only first level bullets.)

5. Select Arial from the Font drop-down list on the Formatting toolbar, and then select 40 from the Font Size drop-down list. Here are the results:

Changing the Bullet Character

While you're at it, why not change the bullet style for the first level bullet? Follow these steps:

1. With the text of the first bulleted item still selected, choose Bullet from the Format menu to display the dialog box shown on the next page.

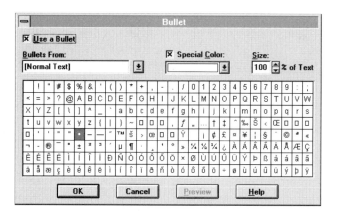

2. Click the arrow at the right end of the Bullets From edit box to display a list of available fonts, and select Wingdings from the bottom of the list to display a new set of characters.

3. Select the right-pointing "twisted arrow" in the sixth row (fourth from the right).

4. Double-click *100* in the Size box, type *80* to reduce the size of the bullet a bit, and then click OK to return to the Slide Master with the new bullet in place, like this:

5. Save TREES.PPT.

Resizing and Repositioning Objects

Earlier, you resized and repositioned the title and subtitle of RECYCLE.PPT's title slide. Using the same techniques, you can resize and reposition objects on the Slide Master so that the changes will affect the entire presentation. Here are the steps:

1. Choose Ruler from the View menu.

2. Click the frame of the selected text object, point to the top center handle, and when the pointer changes to a two headed arrow, drag down until the marker on the vertical ruler is at the 1-inch mark.

3. Click the title object, click the object's frame to select it, point to the top of the frame (not one of the handles), and drag down until the marker on the vertical ruler is at the 3-inch mark.

4. Choose Ruler from the View menu to turn off the rulers.

Adding the Date and Page Number

As you were working your way through the Pick A Look Wizard's dialog boxes at the beginning of the chapter, we mentioned that we would add the date and page number at a later time. Well, the time is now, so with the Slide Master open on your screen, follow these steps:

1. Click anywhere outside the Slide Master to be sure that no objects are currently selected.

2. Choose Date from the Insert menu to insert the date placeholder (a frame with two forward slashes), like this:

Inserting the date

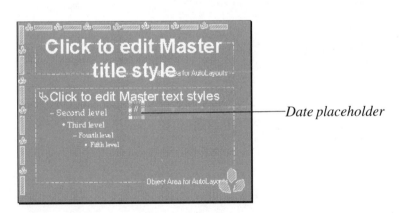

Date placeholder

When you insert the date, time, or page number via the Insert menu, PowerPoint displays a placeholder for each item until you actually print the presentation or view it as a slide show. (For more information about printing, see page 24. For more information about slide shows, see Chapter 7.)

3. Point to the date placeholder's frame (not one of the handles), hold down the left mouse button, and drag the placeholder to the bottom left corner of the Slide Master. Dashed boxes representing the frame and the date indicate where the date placeholder will appear when you release the mouse button.

Inserting page numbers

4. Next, click anywhere outside the Slide Master to deselect the date placeholder, and then choose Page Number from the Insert menu to insert a page number placeholder (a frame with two # signs) on the Slide Master.

5. Repeat step 3, but this time, position the page number placeholder in the top right corner of the Slide Master, which now looks like this:

Page number placeholder

6. Save TREES.PPT one last time, and then choose Close from the File menu.

Now for the really exciting stuff. Follow the steps below to apply your new template to the RECYCLE.PPT presentation:

1. Choose RECYCLE.PPT from the bottom of the File menu. (If RECYCLE.PPT is not one of the four most recently used files, its name won't appear at the bottom of the File menu, and you'll have to use the Open command instead. Click the Open button on the Standard toolbar, and locate and double-click RECYCLE.PPT.)

2. With RECYCLE.PPT on your screen, click the Template button at the bottom of the window, be sure the SLDSHOW directory is open, and then double-click TREES.PPT. Presto! Here's the result:

Adjusting placeholders

You can check the position and size of the date, time (if present), and page number placeholders by clicking the Slide Show button at the bottom of the Presentation window and viewing your slides in Slide Show view. Then to resize a placeholder, return to Slide view by pressing the Esc key, choose Master and then Slide Master from the View menu, and drag the handles around the placeholder's frame in the desired direction. For example, if the date is breaking across two lines, you can increase the size of the placeholder frame so that it fits on a single line, by dragging one of the frame's side handles. To reposition a placeholder, drag its frame (not a handle).

It's as simple as that. (Notice that the company name has disappeared from the bottom left corner of the slide because the name is not part of the TREES.PPT template.)

Before you leave this section about customizing, you need to make a few changes to the color scheme.

Changing the Color Scheme

In PowerPoint, you can change the color scheme of an entire presentation or just a single slide. You can even change the color of specific elements on a slide, such as the title and the background. As you've already seen, you can make changes to an entire presentation through the Slide Master, and you can save those changes in a template to be used over and over again. We'll show you how to change the colors of some elements in the TREES.PPT template that you just created. You can then reapply the template to the RECYCLE.PPT presentation. We'll also show you how to change the color scheme of a single slide.

Before you actually change any colors, you should make the acquaintance of the Slide Color Scheme dialog box. Follow these steps:

1. Close RECYCLE.PPT, being sure to save your changes. Then click the Open button on the Standard toolbar and double-click TREES.PPT.

2. Choose Slide Color Scheme from the Format menu to open the Slide Color Scheme dialog box, shown on the next page.

The effect of color

The colors you use in your presentations are just as important as the fonts you use. Like fonts, different colors can send different messages to your audience. For example, cool colors such as green, blue, and violet are associated with oceans and pastoral settings and can imply peace and tranquillity. Warm colors such as red, orange, and yellow, on the other hand, are associated with fire and can imply aggression and intensity. In RECYCLE.PPT, we use a cool color (blue) to suggest environmental sensitivity and a warm color (red) to suggest environmental insensitivity. In addition to the various moods colors can create, you also need to be aware of these factors when selecting colors for a presentation:

- Cool colors tend to recede from the audience and work best as background colors, while warm colors tend to advance toward the audience and work best at calling attention to specific items.
- Use colors that are complementary, such as orange type on a blue background.
- When creating slides, be sure to use a dark background.
- Avoid placing red and green next to each other. (People who are color blind may not be able to distinguish between these colors.)
- Use color to highlight data. For example, format positive numbers in blue and negative numbers in red.

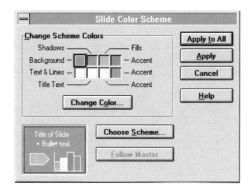

The diagram in the Change Scheme Colors section of the dialog box depicts the colors of the various elements on the current slide. As you'll see in a moment, you can click an element's corresponding color box and then click the Change Color button to change the color of that element. Below is a table describing the elements affected by the eight color boxes in the diagram.

The slide elements

Color box	Affected elements
Background	Slide background.
Text & Lines	Bulleted text and text entered with the text tool. Also, lines and arrows drawn with the line tool and the outlines for AutoShapes and objects drawn with any of the drawing tools.
Shadows	Shadows created with the Shadow command.
Title Text	Slide titles.
Fills	Interior of AutoShapes and objects drawn with the drawing tools. Also, the first series in a graph.
Accent	Second color in graphs, organization charts, and other added elements.
Accent	Third color in graphs, organization charts, and other added elements.
Accent	Fourth color in graphs, organization charts, and other added elements.

Now let's see how the TREES.PPT template looks in a nice, crisp navy blue:

1. Click the Choose Scheme button in the Slide Color Scheme dialog box to display this dialog box:

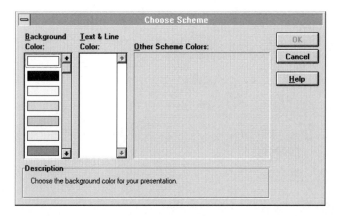

2. Scroll down the Background Color list to see the available colors, and select the darkest blue in the list. PowerPoint then displays a list of colors in the Text & Lines Color list.

Changing the background color

3. Select white in the Text & Lines Color list. Four possible color combinations then appear in the Other Scheme Colors box, like this:

Changing the text and line color

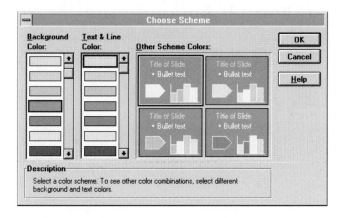

You can view other color combinations by selecting different background and text colors.

4. Click the second color combination in the top row, and then click OK to return to the Slide Color Scheme dialog box.

Now try changing the colors of some specific elements by following these steps:

1. In the Change Scheme Colors section, click the Title Text Color box, which should be yellow, and then click the Change Color button to display the dialog box shown on the next page.

Changing the title text color

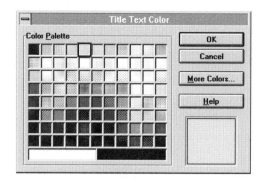

2. Select white (the large rectangle in the bottom left corner), and click OK.

Changing the fill color →

3. Next, click the Fills color box, click Change Color, and then double-click the yellow square in the top row of the Fill Color dialog box.

Applying the new color scheme to the template →

4. Finally, click the Apply To All button to apply the new color scheme to the entire template. (If you click Apply, only the current slide is affected.)

5. Choose Close from the File menu, and when PowerPoint asks if you want to save your changes, click Yes.

Now let's see the effect of the new color scheme on the RECYCLE.PPT presentation:

Reapplying an edited template →

1. Open RECYCLE.PPT, and click the Template button at the bottom of the Presentation window to display the Presentation Template dialog box.

Creating a custom color scheme

You aren't restricted to PowerPoint's predefined color schemes. You can create your own color schemes by first opening a template or an existing presentation and then choosing the Slide Color Scheme command from the Format menu. When the Slide Color Scheme dialog box appears, select one of the color boxes in the Change Scheme Colors section, and click the Change Color button. In the next dialog box, click the More Colors button to display the More Colors dialog box. Here you can create your own colors by dragging the cross-hair pointer to new locations in the large color box on the left. To increase or decrease the intensity of the current color, move the small triangle pointer up or down the bar to the right of the color box. You can also change the values in the Hue, Sat (for *saturation*), and Lum (for *luminance*) or Red, Green, and Blue edit boxes to create a new color. To see the new color, check the Color box in the bottom left corner of the More Colors dialog box. When the color is to your satisfaction, click OK twice to return to the Slide Color Scheme dialog box, where you can then select another color box in the Change Scheme Colors section and repeat the procedure until the new color scheme is complete. Finally, click Apply To All to apply the color scheme to the entire presentation, or click Apply to apply the color scheme to the current slide only.

2. Be sure the SLDSHOW directory is open, and then double-click TREES.PPT to apply it to the recycling presentation.

3. Click the Slide Sorter View button so that you can see all your slides at once, as shown here:

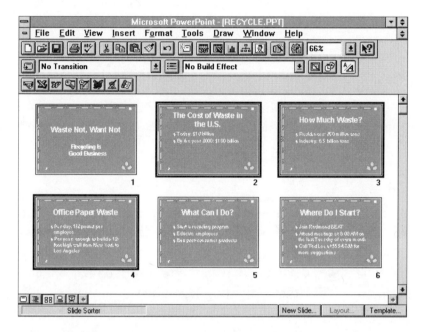

Looks pretty good, doesn't it? Earlier in the chapter, we mentioned that color could affect the mood of your presentation. Let's put this idea to the test by changing the background of Slides 2, 3, and 4, which present some alarming facts, to a fiery red while leaving the other slides bucolic blue. Follow the steps on the next page.

The Slide Background dialog box

Here's another way to change the background color. Select the slide or slides you want to change (or open the Slide Master), and choose Slide Background from the Format menu to display the Slide Background dialog box. Then click the Change Color button at the bottom of the dialog box, and select a new color from the Background Color dialog box. (You can also click the More Colors button, and follow the procedure outlined in the tip on page 52 to create a custom background color.) In addition to the color, you can make other changes to the background via the Slide Background dialog box. For example, you can hide all the objects on the background by deselecting the Display Objects On This Slide option. You can also add shading to the background by first selecting an option in the Shade Styles section of the dialog box and then selecting one of the shading variations in the Variants section. While you're at it, you can darken or lighten your shading selection by adjusting the scroll box in the scroll bar below the Variants section. To implement your background color and shading selections, click the Apply To All or Apply button.

Changing the color of individual slides

1. While still in Slide Sorter view, click Slide 2 to select it. Then hold down the Shift key, and click Slide 3 and Slide 4 to select those slides as well.

2. Choose Slide Color Scheme from the Format menu, and when the Slide Color Scheme dialog box appears, select the Background color box in the Change Scheme Colors section.

3. Click the Change Color button, select the red square in the sixth row of the second column, and click OK.

4. Back at the Slide Color Scheme dialog box, click the Apply button to apply the new background color to the selected slides only.

5. Save RECYCLE.PPT.

Looking at your presentation in Slide Sorter view, you can see the sharp contrast between the slides with blue backgrounds and those with red backgrounds. You have to admit, the blue slides definitely have a more positive feel to them. Remember, like the formatting techniques you learned earlier, you can use color to your advantage—to create certain moods or to play up some topics and downplay others. Take time on your own to investigate PowerPoint's color palette, and if you're not satisfied with the program's predefined colors, create your own (see the tip on page 52).

Preparing the Slide File

The simplest way to output your presentation as a set of 35mm slides is to entrust the imaging procedure to Genigraphics Corporation, a graphics service bureau with seven offices around the country (when this book was written). You prepare your presentation file for outputting as slides by "printing" the file using the Genigraphics Driver that is shipped with PowerPoint. (This driver was automatically transferred to your hard drive if you selected the Complete/Custom option when you ran the PowerPoint or Microsoft Office Setup program. If you cannot locate the driver in step 1 of the instructions on the facing page, run Setup again, and click the Add/Remove button. In the Maintenance Mode dialog box, use the Down Arrow key to highlight Tools but don't deselect

Returning to the master color scheme

If you apply a new color scheme to the current slide only by clicking the Apply button in the Slide Color Scheme dialog box, you can always return that slide to the original, or *master*, color scheme by clicking the Follow Master button in the Slide Color Scheme dialog box. However, if you apply a color scheme to an entire presentation by clicking the Apply To All button, that color scheme becomes the new master color scheme, and clicking the Follow Master button simply reverts any subsequent color changes to the new master rather than to the original color scheme.

its check box, and click the Change Options button. Then select the Genigraphics Driver And GraphicsLink option, click OK, and click Continue to proceed with installation.)

Here are the steps for preparing your file:

1. Choose Print from the File menu, click the Printer button, and in the Print Setup dialog box, select Genigraphics Driver on GENI, and click OK. Then click OK in the Print dialog box.

2. On the Genigraphics Job Instructions dialog box, enter the requested information, and click OK. PowerPoint prints your presentation to a file in the WINDOWS\SYSTEM\GENI directory using the Genigraphics Driver, which warns you of any problems it encounters. When the printing process is complete, you see the Genigraphics Billing Information dialog box.

3. Enter your billing information, and click OK.

   If you specified that you want to send the file to Genigraphics via modem, you can now double-click the GraphicsLink icon in Program Manager to send the file to the Genigraphics facility in Memphis, which will process your order and send it back to you. (You will need to customize the communications settings for your modem by choosing Communications Setup from the File menu.) If you specified that you want to create a file on disk, you can copy the file to a disk and either take it or mail it to the nearest Genigraphics facility. (Call 1-800-638-7348 to get the appropriate address and phone number.)

Power of Persuasion: Adding Graphs

We changed the layout of Slide 2 of RECYCLE.PPT
to the Text & Graph AutoLayout, entered the graph's data in
Microsoft Graph, and formatted the graph.
Then we used the Insert Graph button to add a graph to Slide 3,
changed the graph type to 3-D pie, and exploded the slices.

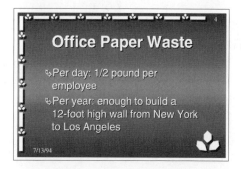

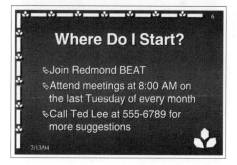

This chapter is all about the real meat and potatoes of presentations: graphs. Words and numbers are nice, but visual representations of your words and numbers can really make an audience sit up and take notice. For example, there's nothing like a good old line graph to show the fluctuations in sales over the past six months.

Microsoft Graph →

As a charter member of Microsoft Office, PowerPoint shares a built-in graphing program, Microsoft Graph, with other Office members. Graph is also included with the stand-alone version of PowerPoint. In this chapter, we show you the ins and outs of using Graph so that you can take full advantage of it for your own presentations. We start off by adding a 3-D column graph to an existing slide, and we show you how to format and manipulate the graph in various ways. Then we work with a 3-D pie graph on a different slide. Finally, we discuss the various graph types. If you've already created graphs in Microsoft Excel, you can use the following section as a refresher course. If you've never worked with Graph before, we'll help you quickly come up to speed.

You can add a graph to an existing slide in one of two ways: by changing the layout of the slide to one that includes a graph placeholder, or by clicking the Insert Graph button on the Standard toolbar (or by choosing Microsoft Graph from the Insert menu). We'll start with the first method.

Using a Graph AutoLayout

Using the RECYCLE.PPT presentation you created in Chapter 2, let's add a graph to Slide 2 by changing its layout:

1. Open RECYCLE.PPT in Slide view, and move to Slide 2.

2. Click the Layout button at the bottom of the Presentation window, and when the Slide Layout dialog box appears, select the Text & Graph AutoLayout (the second AutoLayout in the second row), and click Apply. Slide 2 now looks like the one shown here:

New graph slides

If you want to create a brand new graph slide instead of adding a graph to an existing slide, you can simply click the New Slide button at the bottom of the Presentation window, select one of the graph AutoLayouts in the New Slide dialog box, and then click OK.

3. Double-click the graph placeholder to start Microsoft Graph.
Your screen looks something like this:

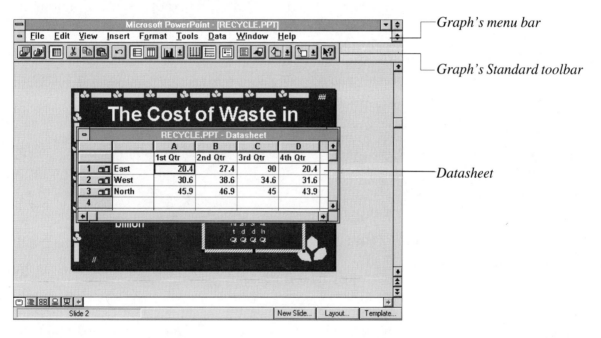

Graph's menu bar

Graph's Standard toolbar

Datasheet

As you can see, Graph first presents you with its default
datasheet, which resembles a worksheet in a speadsheet
program. In the topmost row and leftmost column of the
datasheet, are column and row headings, or *labels*. You can
edit and format these labels like any other text in PowerPoint.
Above the column labels and to the right of the row labels are
column letter and row number buttons. Depending on
whether your data is organized by column or by row (see the
tip on page 60), markers appear on the column letter or row

The datasheet

number buttons to indicate the current graph type. To select an entire column or row, simply click the corresponding button. To select the entire datasheet, click the "blank" button located at the intersection of the column letter and row number buttons.

Cells →

Moving around the datasheet →

Gridlines divide the datasheet into units called *cells*. You enter the data for your graph by first clicking a cell to select it and then typing the information. To move to another cell, click it with the mouse; use the Arrow keys; or press Enter (to move to the cell below), Tab (to move to the next cell), or Shift+Tab (to move to the previous cell). You can also press Home or End to move to the beginning or end of the current row, or Ctrl+Home or Ctrl+End to move to the beginning or end of the datasheet.

Now that you're acquainted with Graph's datasheet, you can replace the "dummy" data with your own recycling information, starting with the labels:

1. Select the first cell in column A (the cell that contains *1st Qtr*) by clicking it with the mouse. (Be careful not to click outside the datasheet or graph. If you do, Graph automatically returns you to PowerPoint. You must then double-click the graph on the current slide to start Graph again.)

2. Type *1994*, move to the first cell in column B, and type *2000*.

3. Select the first cell in row 1 (the cell that contains *East*), and type *U.S.*

4. Now press Enter to move to the first cell in row 2, and type *Europe*.

5. Press Enter one more time, and type *Japan*.

To speed up the entry of the remaining data in the datasheet, try this technique:

1. Point to the second cell in column A, hold down the left mouse button, drag to the third cell in column B, and then release the mouse button. The datasheet should look like this:

By row or by column

You can arrange the data series in your datasheet by row or by column. Graph assumes that the series are arranged by row; but if you have arranged the series by column, you can ensure that Graph will plot your data correctly by clicking the By Column button on Graph's Standard toolbar. If you want to return to the by-row arrangement, click the By Row button. Graph places miniature markers on the row number buttons of the datasheet if the data series are arranged by row and on the column letter buttons if the data series are arranged by column.

RECYCLE.PPT - Datasheet				
	A	**B**	**C**	**D**
	1994	2000	3rd Qtr	4th Qtr
1 U.S.	20.4	27.4	90	20.4
2 Europe	30.6	38.6	34.6	31.6
3 Japan	45.9	46.9	45	43.9
4				

2. Now type *10*, press Enter, type *6*, press Enter, type *7.5*, and press Enter. In the next column, type the data shown below, pressing Enter after each number:

100
57
75

(By the way, this data is ficticious and is used for demonstration purposes only.)

3. Choose Save from Graph's File menu to save your work. (We won't tell you to save from this point on, but you should remember to save often as you work through the chapter.)

Now you can plot the graph. You don't want to plot the "dummy" data in columns C and D, so first exclude it by following these steps:

1. Click the column letter button for column C, hold down the Shift key, click the column letter button for column D, and release the Shift key.

Excluding data

2. With both columns selected, choose Exclude Row/Col from Graph's Data menu. Now the datasheet looks like this:

RECYCLE.PPT - Datasheet				
	A	**B**	**C**	**D**
	1994	2000	3rd Qtr	4th Qtr
1 U.S.	10	100	90	20.4
2 Europe	6	57	34.6	31.6
3 Japan	7.5	80	45	43.9
4				

3. Click the View Datasheet button on Graph's Standard toolbar or choose the Datasheet command from Graph's View menu to remove the datasheet. The new graph looks like the one shown on the next page.

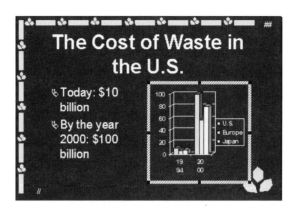

Changing the graph type

If Graph does not plot a 3-D column graph when you click the View Datasheet button, you can use the Chart Type button on Graph's Standard toolbar to select the type of graph you want to plot. When you click the Chart Type button, Graph displays a "tear-off" palette of the 14 basic graph types—two-dimensional and three-dimensional—so that you can simply click the type you want. As its name suggests, the Chart Type palette can be "torn off", or separated, from Graph's Standard toolbar. To tear off the palette, position the mouse pointer over the palette's border, hold down the left mouse button, and drag the palette to a new location in the Graph window. A close box and title bar then appear at the top of the Chart Type palette. To remove the palette from the window, click the close box. To return the palette to the toolbar or move it elsewhere in the window, drag its title bar.

Obviously, you'll have to make some adjustments, such as fixing the category (x) axis labels and repositioning the graph. As you read through the next few pages, you'll discover that Graph offers many different ways for you to adjust and modify graphs so that you get just the right look.

Working with Graph Objects

Before you can make any adjustments to a graph, you must select the graph object you want to change. If Graph is still open, you can select a graph object by simply clicking it with the mouse. Handles then surround the object to indicate that it is selected. If you are working in PowerPoint, you can quickly start Graph by double-clicking the current graph or by clicking the graph once and pressing Enter. You can then click the graph object you want to modify.

After you select a graph object, choose the corresponding *Selected* command from Graph's Format menu to open a Format dialog box with options related to the selected object. You can also open the Format dialog box by simply double-clicking the graph object.

If you're a little baffled by all this, don't worry: We'll walk you through the entire process in a moment. Before we do, however, take a minute or two to study the following figure, which depicts the graph objects on a typical graph:

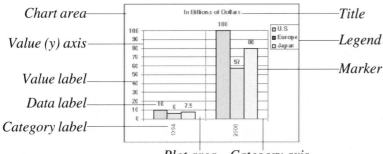

Chart area — Title
Value (y) axis — Legend
Value label — Marker
Data label
Category label

Plot area   Category axis

Adding and Formatting a Title

You can add a title to the graph, the category (x) axis, the value (y) axis, or all three by choosing the Titles command from Graph's Insert menu. You can then format the title or titles using the Format dialog box. Try adding a title to the column graph in RECYCLE.PPT now:

1. Be sure Graph is open. (If it isn't, double-click the column graph on Slide 2 to start the program.

2. Choose the Titles command from Graph's Insert menu to display this dialog box:

3. Select the Chart Title option, and click OK. Graph adds a title placeholder to the chart area.

4. Double-click the placeholder text to select it, type *In Billions of Dollars*, and click anywhere outside the graph's frame to enter the title.

5. Now point to the title, and click once to select it. Graph surrounds the title with a frame and handles.

6. Choose Selected Chart Title from Graph's Format menu to display the dialog box shown on the next page.

Adding an axis title

To add a title to a graph's axis, choose Titles from Graph's Insert menu, select the appropriate option in the Titles dialog box, and click OK. Then, when the axis title placeholder appears, type the text of the title. If you want to rotate the title, first select it, and choose Selected Axis Title from Graph's Format menu. Next, click the Alignment tab of the Format Axis Title dialog box, and select one of the options in the Orientation section.

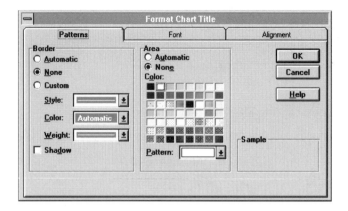

7. Click the Alignment tab, select the Top option in the Vertical section, and click OK. The title shifts upward to give you a little more room.

As you continue to make changes to the graph objects, you'll notice similarities between the Format dialog boxes. For example, just about every dialog box offers a Patterns tab containing options for adding, removing, and formatting borders, as well as changing the color or adding a pattern to the selected graph object. After you become familiar with two or three of the Format dialog boxes, you'll have no trouble working your way through the others.

Changing the Color of a Data Series

You may recall from Chapter 2 that when you selected a new color scheme, PowerPoint assigned colors to three Accent elements (see page 49). Along with the Fills color, the Accent colors are used in the data series markers of graphs. The first data series in the sample column graph is assigned the Fills color, the second series is assigned the first Accent color, the third series is assigned the second Accent color, and so on.

You don't have to use the colors of the selected color scheme, however. You can change the color of an entire data series or of an individual marker in the series using the Format dialog box. Here's how:

Color and Pattern buttons

To quickly add color or a pattern to any graph object, select the object, click the Color or Pattern button on Graph's Standard toolbar, and select the desired color or pattern.

1. Click either of the Europe markers to select that series of data. Handles appear on both markers. (If you want to select only a single marker in a data series, click the marker once to select the entire series, and then click the desired marker.)

2. Choose Selected Data Series from Graph's Format menu to display this dialog box:

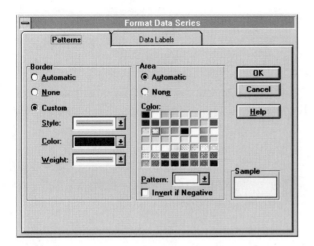

3. In the Area section on the Patterns tab, select the third blue box in the second row of the Color palette, and click OK. The light blue marker for Europe is now dark blue. (In the legend, note that the legend key—the small color box—for Europe changes accordingly.)

Adding and Formatting Legends

By default, Graph added a legend to the column graph in RECYCLE.PPT. If your graph does not have a legend, you can add one by clicking the Legend button on Graph's Standard toolbar or by choosing the Legend command from Graph's Insert menu. You can remove a legend by selecting it and pressing the Delete key.

Because a legend is a graph object, you can format it using the same techniques described for titles and data series markers. First select the legend, and then choose Selected Legend from Graph's Format menu, or double-click the legend. When the Format Legend dialog box appears, use the options on the Patterns, Font, and Placement tabs to change the border, background, font, and location of the legend.

You can also select an entry in a legend (such as *Europe* in the sample column graph's legend), and change its font, font style, size, and so on using the Format Legend Entry dialog box. And if that's not enough, you can even select a legend key (the small color box next to each legend entry), and

Formatting legend entries and keys

Scaling axes

You can use the options on the Scale tab of the Format Axis dialog box to change the scale of a graph's axes. For the value (y) axis, change the default end points of the scale by changing the settings in the Minimum and Maximum edit boxes. Change the position of major and minor tick marks by changing the settings in the Major Unit and Minor Unit edit boxes. In addition, you can scale the value axis logarithmically (as opposed to linearly) so that each tick mark represents a power of 10. For the category (x) axis, change the intervals between tick-mark labels and tick marks by changing the settings in the corresponding Number Of Categories edit boxes. You can also specify that the value axis intersect the category axis between categories. For both the value axis and the category axis, indicate where you want the axes to intersect by selecting one of the Crosses At options. In addition, you can specify that the order of either axis be reversed. If you reverse the value axis, the graph is then turned upside down so that the highest values are at the bottom of the axis and the lowest values are at the top, which is helpful if your graph's values are negative. If you reverse the category axis, the categories are inverted so that the first category is last and the last category is first, which is helpful if you want to focus on the last category. If your graph is three-dimensional, you can also scale the series (y) axis in similar ways.

change its border, color, and background using the Format Legend Key dialog box.

As well as using the Placement tab of the Format Legend dialog box to reposition and resize the legend, you can use the mouse. Try this:

1. Click the legend once to select it. (Be sure the entire legend is selected, not one of the legend entries or keys.)

2. Point to the border surrounding the legend (not a handle), hold down the left mouse button, drag upward until the legend is positioned just below and to the right of the graph's title, and release the mouse button.

3. Click anywhere in the chart area to deselect the legend. (Be careful not to click *outside* the chart area, or you'll wind up back in PowerPoint.) The graph now looks like this:

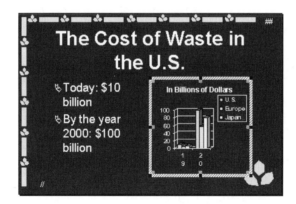

Adding and Formatting Axes, Tick Marks, Gridlines, and Labels

The two-dimensional column graph in RECYCLE.PPT has two axes: the *value* or vertical y axis and the *category* or horizontal x axis. Logically, values are plotted along the value axis, and categories are plotted along the category axis. You'll find axes in all the graph types except pie and doughnut graphs (see page 77 for a description of graph types), which do not have axes. Some three-dimensional graph types, such as three-dimensional area, three-dimensional column, three-dimensional line, and three-dimensional surface graphs, have a third axis, called the *series* axis. In these graphs, the x axis remains the category axis, the y axis becomes the series axis, and the z axis becomes the value axis.

This may all sound a bit confusing, but the figures shown below should help clarify matters. The figure on the left is a two-dimensional column graph with category (x) and value (y) axes. The figure on the right is a three-dimensional column graph with category (x), series (y), and value (z) axes. Note that the three-dimensional column graph has additional graph objects called the walls and the floor and that the value axis rises up from the floor while the category and series axes are plotted along the floor.

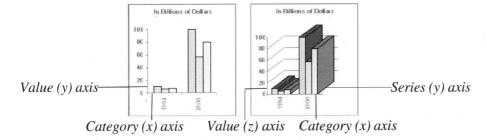

Value (y) axis ___ *Series (y) axis*

Category (x) axis   *Value (z) axis*   *Category (x) axis*

Follow the steps below to change the color of both axes in the sample column graph:

1. Select either axis by clicking it with the mouse.

2. Choose Selected Axis from Graph's Format menu to display the Format Axis dialog box.

3. In the Axis section of the Patterns tab, click the arrow to the right of the Color edit box, select the third blue box in the second row of the Color palette, and click OK.

4. Repeat steps 1 through 3 for the remaining axis.

The small marks used to group values or categories along the axes are called *tick marks*. A graph can have major tick marks and minor tick marks, but only major tick marks appear by default. To add minor tick marks, select the axis, choose Selected Axis from Graph's Format menu, and then select one of the Minor Tick Mark Type options on the Patterns tab of the Format Axis dialog box. You can also use options on the Patterns tab to remove or reposition the major tick marks along the selected axis.

Remodeling the walls and the floor

You can format the walls and the floor in a three-dimensional graph just as you format other graph objects. Simply select the walls or floor with the mouse, and choose the corresponding Selected command from Graph's Format menu. When the Format dialog box appears, you can use the options on the Patterns tab to change the border and area of the walls or floor.

In some cases, gridlines can help make a graph more readable. The current graph has gridlines emanating from the major tick marks along the value axis, allowing you to more easily assess the values of the data markers. You can add gridlines to both major and minor tick marks by choosing Gridlines from Graph's Insert menu and selecting options in the Gridlines dialog box. (To quickly add gridlines to the major tick marks only, click the Vertical Gridlines and/or Horizontal Gridlines buttons on Graph's Standard toolbar.) After you've added gridlines, you can format them by selecting a gridline along one axis, choosing Selected Gridlines from Graph's Format menu, and then using the Patterns tab of the Format Gridlines dialog box to change the style, color, and weight of all the gridlines or the Scale tab to change the scale. (For more information about changing the scale, see the tip on page 66.) If you want to remove gridlines from your graph, either click the Vertical and/or Horizontal Gridlines button or choose Gridlines from Graph's Insert menu and deselect the appropriate options.

The column graph in RECYCLE.PPT sports tick-mark labels along both axes. You can change the position (see the adjacent tip), font, number format (see the tip on page 69), and alignment of tick-mark labels by selecting their corresponding axis, choosing Selected Axis from Graph's Format menu, and then selecting options in the Format Axis dialog box.

For example, to fix the alignment of the labels along the category axis, follow these steps:

1. Click the category (x) axis, and choose Selected Axis from Graph's Format menu.

2. When the Format Axis dialog box appears, click the Alignment tab.

3. In the Orientation section, select the second vertical option, and click OK. Here is the result:

Changing label position

By default, Graph places tick-mark labels next to their respective axes. You can change the position of the labels by selecting one of the Tick-Mark Labels options on the Patterns tab of the Format Axes dialog box. Selecting the Low or High option places labels next to the minimum or maximum values of the other axis, respectively. Selecting the None option removes the labels altogether.

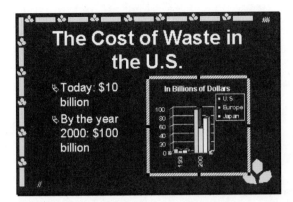

4. The labels don't quite fit, so select the chart area, and drag the bottom center handle down a bit. (Refer to the figure on page 63 if you need help locating the chart area.)

Formatting the Chart and Plot Areas

To give the chart area a little more distinction, you can add a border to it and change its background color. (You can use the same techniques to format the plot area.) And, rather than change the formatting of individual text elements on the graph, such as the title and tick-mark labels, you can save yourself some time by changing the fomatting of all the text at once in the Format Chart Area dialog box. Follow these steps to add a border, change the background color, and format the text of the column graph in RECYCLE.PPT:

1. With Graph open and the chart area selected, choose Selected Chart Area from Graph's Format menu. Graph displays the Format Chart Area dialog box.

2. On the Patterns tab, click the arrow to the right of the Color edit box in the Border section to display the Color palette, and then select the third blue box in the second row of the palette.

3. Next, click the arrow to the right of the Weight edit box, and select the last option (heavy).

4. Now click the Shadow check box to add a shadow to the border.

Formatting numbers

To change the formatting of numeric tick-mark labels, you can use the options on the Number tab of the Format Axis dialog box. If the Linked To Source option is selected, the numbers have the same formatting as the numbers in the datasheet. To apply a different format, select an option from the Category list, and then select the format you want from the Format Codes list. A sample of your selection appears at the bottom of the Number tab. You can create a custom format by selecting the Custom option in the Category list and entering the appropriate codes in the Code edit box. (For more details about these codes, see this topic in PowerPoint's on-line Help system.)

5. To change the color of the chart area's background, move to the Area section of the Patterns tab, and select the white box in the first row of the Color palette.

Adding text boxes and arrows

To embellish your graph with text, click the Text Box button on Graph's Standard toolbar, position the cross-hair pointer where you want the text box to appear, hold down the left mouse button, and drag to create the text box. A flashing insertion point appears inside the text box so that you can enter the text, and as you type, the text automatically wraps within the invisible boundaries of the box. To reposition a text box, place the mouse pointer on the text box's border, hold down the left mouse button, and drag the box to a new location. To resize a text box, drag one of its handles. To delete a text box, select it and press Delete.

You can also connect a text box to an item in your graph by drawing an arrow. Click the Drawing button on Graph's Standard toolbar to display the Drawing toolbar. Then click the Arrow button, position the mouse pointer at the starting point for the arrow, hold down the left mouse button, and drag to the ending point for the arrow.

Like other graph objects, you can format text boxes and arrows by using the options in the Format Object dialog box.

6. Finally, to change the color of all the text on the graph, click the Font tab to display these options in the Format Chart Area dialog box:

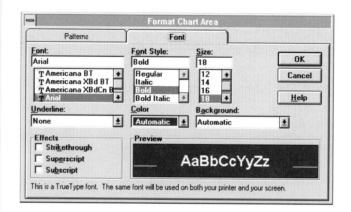

7. Click the arrow to the right of the Color edit box, select the third blue box in the second row of the drop-down Color palette, and click OK to close the dialog box.

Now that you've added a border to the graph, the labels along the category axis might be a bit crowded. You can adjust the position of the plot area to fix this problem. Here are the steps:

1. Click between 1994 and 2000 to select the plot area (refer to the figure on page 63 if you need help locating the plot area).

2. Point to the frame surrounding the plot area (not a handle), hold down the left mouse button, and when the positioning box appears, drag upward just enough to move the category-axis labels away from the graph's bottom border.

3. Click anywhere *outside* the chart area to return to PowerPoint, and then click anywhere outside Slide 2 to deselect the graph. Here are the results:

Moving and Sizing Graphs in PowerPoint

You don't have to open Microsoft Graph in order to move and resize the chart area of a graph. You can accomplish these tasks in PowerPoint, like this:

1. Click the column graph in RECYCLE.PPT to select it.

2. Point anywhere inside the graph's border, hold down the left mouse button, and when the dashed positioning box appears, drag to the left about 1/2 inch.

3. To increase the height of the graph, point to the bottom center handle, and when the pointer changes to a double-headed arrow, hold down the left mouse button, and drag down until the bottom border of the graph aligns with the bottom of the leaves graphic.

4. Deselect the graph to see these results:

Creating picture graphs

To substitute pictures for the markers in a two-dimensional graph, select a picture from another application, such as Paintbrush, and copy it to the Windows Clipboard. Activate the graph, select the series of markers you want to replace, and click the Paste button on Graph's Standard toolbar or choose Paste from Graph's Edit menu. In bar and column graphs, the pictures are stretched to fill the markers. You can stack the pictures instead by selecting the Stack option on the Patterns tab of the Format Data Point dialog box.

Using the Insert Graph Button

As we mentioned at the beginning of this chapter, PowerPoint offers two ways to add a graph to an existing slide. The first method, which we've already covered, involves using a graph AutoLayout. The second method, which we'll cover here, involves using the Insert Graph button on PowerPoint's Standard toolbar. While we're at it, we'll also take this opportunity to introduce you to Graph's chart types so that you can get a feel for when you would use different types of graphs.

Follow the steps below to add a 3-D pie graph to Slide 3 of RECYCLE.PPT:

1. With RECYCLE.PPT open in Slide view, move to Slide 3.

2. Click the Insert Graph button on the Standard toolbar (or choose Microsoft Graph from the Insert menu).

3. When the default datasheet appears, complete it as shown here, and use the Exclude Row/Col command on Graph's Data menu to exclude rows 2 and 3 and column D from the graph (see page 61). We used the mouse to widen column A so that the entire Residential heading is visible (see the tip on page 73 for more information).

		A	B	C	D
		Residential	Industrial	Other	4th Qtr
1	Waste	0.85	6.5	2.65	20.4
2	West	30.6	38.6	34.6	31.6
3	North	45.9	46.9	45	43.9
4					

RECYCLE.PPT - Datasheet

4. In this case, we don't want to use the default column graph type, so click the Chart Type button on Graph's Standard toolbar to display this palette of options:

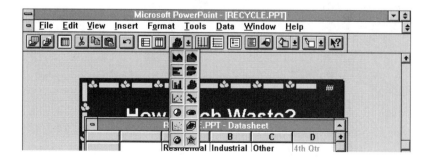

5. Click the 3-D pie icon (the fifth icon in the right column).

6. Now click the View Datasheet button on Graph's Standard toolbar. The 3-D pie graph looks like this:

7. Point to the top center handle, and drag down until the graph no longer obscures the bulleted text.

Adding Data Labels

In addition to the labels along the axes in graphs, you can add labels to the data series markers themselves. These labels can even show the value or percent of each marker and can include the legend key. As with other graph objects, you can format data labels by selecting a label or labels, choosing Selected Data Labels from Graph's Format menu, and then selecting options in the Format Data Labels dialog box, which is similar to the other Format dialog boxes you have seen so far.

Follow the steps below to add data labels to the pie graph:

1. Select the legend, and press the Delete key. (The data labels you're going to add will make the legend redundant.)

2. Choose Data Labels from Graph's Insert menu to display this dialog box:

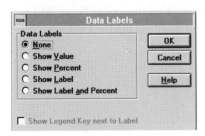

Adjusting column width

To increase or decrease the width of a column in a datasheet, select the column (click the corresponding column letter button), choose Column Width from Graph's Format menu, and enter a number in the Column Width dialog box. Click the Best Fit button in the Column Width dialog box to automatically adjust the column width to fit the longest entry in the column. You can also use the mouse to change the column width. Simply point to the border that separates adjacent column letter buttons, and when the pointer changes to a vertical bar with two arrows, hold down the left mouse button and drag to the left or right. If you double-click the border between two column letter buttons, the width of the column on the left is automatically adjusted to fit the longest entry. You can select multiple columns, and use any of the methods described above to change the width of all the selected columns simultaneously.

3. Select the Show Label And Percent option, and click OK.

The plot area of the pie graph has been reduced to accommodate the labels, which now appear next to their respective data markers. Increase the size of the plot area, and then reposition the data labels by following these steps:

1. Click the plot area to select it, point to the bottom right handle, and drag downward.

2. Drag the other corner handles until the graph has approximately doubled in size.

3. Now click the Industrial label to select it, point to its frame, and drag the label until it's touching its marker.

4. Repeat step 3, dragging the other two labels to their respective markers, like this:

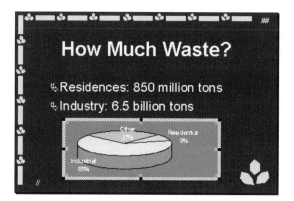

Separating Slices

In pie graphs and on the outer ring of doughnut graphs, you can separate the individual markers, or slices, by simply dragging them with the mouse. As you'll see if you follow these steps, separating the slices helps to distinguish them:

1. Click the Residential marker to select it. (Selecting individual markers is often a tricky process. You know when a single marker is selected because it's the only one surrounded by handles.)

2. Point to the marker, and drag away from the center of the pie.

Adjusting the viewing angle

You can use the options in the Format 3-D View dialog box to change the elevation, rotation, and height of a 3-D graph. To access this dialog box, choose 3-D View from Graph's Format menu. For 3-D area, column, line, and surface graphs, you can also use the mouse to change the elevation and rotation. Just click a corner of the graph to display handles at all the corners, and then drag one of the corner handles up or down to change the elevation or left or right to change the rotation.

3. Repeat step 2 for the Industrial data marker. Here's what the graph looks like after you return to PowerPoint:

Graph Types

No matter what type of graph you need—column, pie, line, and so on—Graph has a format that will probably do the job. You can always come up with impressive visual support for a presentation by carefully selecting from among Power-Point's many predefined graph types. As you have seen, when a graph or its datasheet is active, you can change the basic graph type by clicking the Chart Type button on Graph's Standard toolbar and selecting from the palette of types. For greater flexibility, you can choose Chart Type from the Format menu and select from the Chart Type dialog box, as follows:

1. With Slide 3 displayed, double-click the pie graph to start Graph, and then choose Chart Type from Graph's Format menu to display this dialog box:

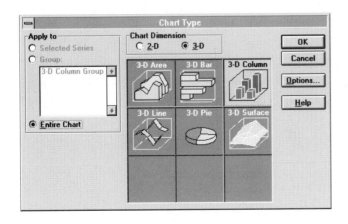

Rotating a pie graph

To rotate a pie graph, choose the 3-D Pie Group command from the bottom of Graph's Format menu or the Format 3-D Pie Group command from the bottom of the shortcut menu. When the Format 3-D Pie Group dialog box appears, click the Options tab, enter the number of degrees you want to rotate the pie in the Angle Of First Slice edit box, and click OK. Your pie graph is displayed at the bottom of the Options tab so that you can see the effects of your changes.

You can select from among 14 basic graph types (8 two-dimensional and 6 three-dimensional) and a wide variety of subtypes.

2. To see the selected graph's subtypes, click the Options button to display this dialog box:

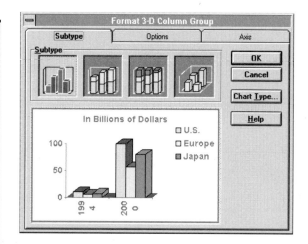

You can also access the Format Group dialog box by choosing the Group command for the current graph type from the bottom of Graph's Format menu or by choosing the Format Group command from the bottom of the shortcut menu.

You can click the Options and Axis tabs to change settings that are specific to the selected graph type. For example, on the Options tab of the Format Column Group dialog box, you can increase or decrease the amount of space between the column markers by changing the setting in the Overlap edit box. On the Options tab of the Format Pie Group dialog box, you won't find an Overlap option, but you will find the Angle Of First Slice option that allows you to rotate the pie graph (see the tip on page 75). A discussion of all the options available in the Format Group dialog box is beyond the scope of this book, but you might want to take some time to explore on your own.

3. Return to the Chart Type dialog box, by clicking the Chart Type button, and then click Cancel to close the dialog box.

The two-dimensional graph types available with Graph include the following:

- Area graphs, which look something like line graphs but which plot multiple data series as cumulative layers with different colors, patterns, or shades.

- Bar graphs, which are ideal for showing the variations in the value of an item over time, or for showing the values of several items at a single point in time.

- Column graphs, which are ideal for showing the variations in the value of an item over time, as with the sample column graph in RECYCLE.PPT. In addition to the simple column graph that you've already seen, you can create stacked or 100 percent stacked column graphs by selecting those subtypes.

- Line graphs, which are often used to show variations in the value of more than one item over time. Two subtypes include high-low-close and open-high-low-close, which are used to show data, such as stock prices, that have high and low values during an interval.

- Pie graphs, which are ideal for showing the percentages of an item that can be assigned to the item's components, as with the sample pie graph in RECYCLE.PPT. (Pie graphs can plot only one data series.)

- XY (scatter) graphs, which are used to detect correlations between independent items (such as a person's weight and height).

- Doughnut graphs, which display the data in a doughnut shape. Similar to the pie graph, they can, however, plot more than one data series.

- Radar graphs, which plot each series on its own axis radiating from a center point.

In addition, you can create three-dimensional area, bar, column, line, pie, and surface graphs. And you can create various combination graphs, which plot one type of graph on top of another as an "overlay" (see the adjacent tip).

Combination graphs

In Graph, you can combine 2-D graph types to create combination graphs. For example, you can plot the fluctuations in interest rates as a line graph and the number of new homes sold within the same time period as a column graph to show the relationship, if any, between the two. The fastest way to create a combination graph is to select one or more series in the current (2-D) graph, click the Chart Type button on Graph's Standard toolbar, and select a different 2-D graph type from the Chart Type palette. (Note that you cannot create combinations of 3-D graphs.) You can also choose the Chart Type command from Graph's Format menu, and select a graph type from the Chart Type dialog box.

After you create a combination graph, you can show the different ranges in values by adding a secondary category and/or value axis to the graph. Choose the Axes command from Graph's Insert menu, and select the desired option(s). Then, to assign a particular graph type to a secondary axis, choose the appropriate Group command from the bottom of the Format or shortcut menu, click the Axis tab, select the Secondary Axis option, and click OK.

4

More Persuasive Power:
Adding Org Charts and Tables

*We added an organization chart to the end of RECYCLE.PPT,
creating and formatting different levels of boxes and lines
to illustrate the structure of the BEAT organization.
Then we used Word's table-making capabilities
to create and format a table on Slide 6 of the presentation.*

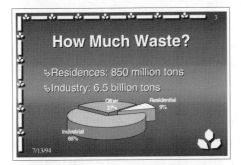

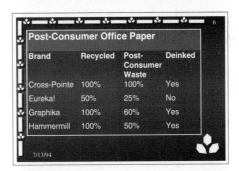

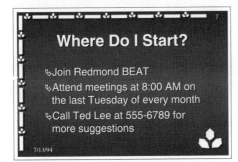

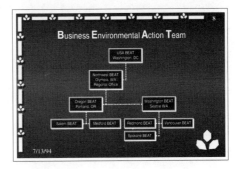

You've seen how to give weight to your arguments by plotting numbers as graphs. But adding graphs to your slides isn't the only way to add visual information to your presentations. In this chapter, we show you how to create and format organization charts to depict management structure. With a little imagination, the basic organization chart elements can also be used to develop flow charts that illustrate processes. We also cover how to create and format tables that you can use to summarize a collection of data. Although you will probably use these two features less frequently than you use Microsoft Graph, after working through the examples in this chapter, you'll be able to find ways to use organization charts and tables so that they contribute to the overall effectiveness of your presentations.

Creating Organization Charts

If you flip back to the previous page, you'll see an organization chart on Slide 8 of the RECYCLE.PPT presentation. As its name suggests, an organization chart organizes information. In this case, the information is organized in a series of boxes connected with lines. Organization charts, henceforth known as *org charts*, are useful for showing hierarchies, such as the executive branch of a corporation where the CEO occupies the top position and a president, vice presidents, and so on, occupy the subordinate positions.

In this section, we'll create an org chart to depict the hierarchy (structure) of USA BEAT, the environmental group from which Redmond BEAT got its start. You'll also learn how to rearrange org charts and how to format their various components. Let's get started:

1. Open RECYCLE.PPT and display Slide 6 in Slide view.

2. Click the New Slide button at the bottom of the Presentation window, and when the New Slide dialog box appears, double-click the Org Chart AutoLayout (the third AutoLayout in the second row) to add Slide 7 to the presentation.

3. Double-click the org chart placeholder in the slide's object area to display a window something like this one:

Adding an org chart to an existing slide

You can add an org chart to an existing slide in one of two ways. The easiest way is to move to the slide in Slide view, and then click the Insert Org Chart button on the Standard toolbar. When the Org Chart window opens, you can complete the org chart as usual. A second, more involved, technique is to use the Object command on the Insert menu. First move to the slide in Slide view, and choose Object from the Insert menu. When the Insert Object dialog box appears, be sure the Create New option is selected, and then double-click the Microsoft Organization Chart 1.0 option in the Object Type list. As before, the Org Chart window opens so that you can complete the org chart.

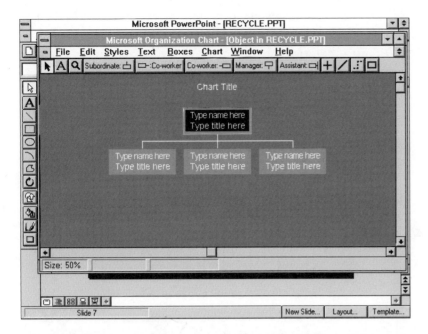

Like Microsoft Graph, Microsoft Organization Chart is a program within a program. As you can see, the Org Chart window has its own menu bar, toolbar, and status bar. You use the menu commands and toolbar buttons to create an org chart and then add it to a PowerPoint slide.

Microsoft Organization Chart

4. Click the Maximize button at the right end of the Org Chart window's title bar to maximize the window.

5. Select the text of the chart title placeholder with the mouse (you may have to scroll the window to see this placeholder), and type *Business Environmental Action Team.*

Adding a title

Now, before you go any further, change the interior color of the org chart's boxes so that you can more easily see the contents. (This step is not always necessary; however, this org chart reflects the color scheme you selected in Chapter 2, and some adjustments are needed here.)

1. Click any of the boxes, hold down the Shift key, and click the remaining boxes to select them.

Changing the color of the boxes

2. Choose Box Color from Org Chart's Boxes menu, and then select black from the drop-down list of colors.

With this detail out of the way, you're ready to fill in the org chart's boxes:

Filling in the boxes

1. Click the topmost box to select it, type *Northwest BEAT* as the name, and press Enter.

2. Type *Olympia, WA* as the title, and press Enter.

3. For the first comment, type *Regional Office*, and then click the leftmost subordinate box to select it.

4. Type *Washington BEAT*, press Enter, and type *Seattle, WA*.

5. Click the second subordinate box, type *Oregon BEAT*, press Enter, type *Portland, OR*, and click outside the box. Here are the results:

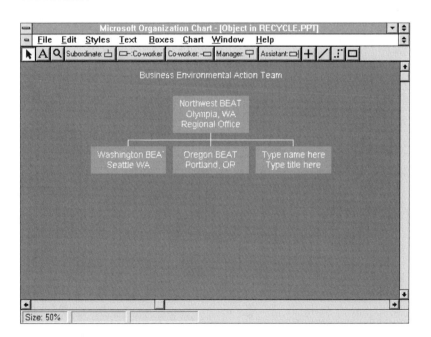

Updating the presentation

6. Choose Update RECYCLE.PPT from the Org Chart's File menu to update the RECYCLE.PPT presentation.

Saving the org chart

In order to actually save the org chart as part of the presentation, you must return to PowerPoint and choose Save from PowerPoint's File menu. Then, to reopen the Org Chart window, you can simply double-click the org chart in PowerPoint. (If you want to save the org chart as a separate file, you can use the Save Copy As command on Org Chart's File menu.) We won't tell you to update or save from this point on, but you should remember to do so often as you work through this chapter.

Adding and Removing Boxes

You aren't limited to the four boxes the Org Chart program has provided. You can add and remove boxes with just a few mouse clicks. Try this:

1. To add a box to the top of the org chart, click the topmost box to select it, click the Manager button on the Org Chart toolbar, move the mouse pointer (which is now shaped like a manager box) to the selected box, and click once.

2. In the new manager box, type *USA BEAT*, press Enter, and type *Washington, DC*.

3. Next, select the Northwest BEAT box, click the Assistant button on the Org Chart toolbar, and then click the Northwest BEAT box to add an assistant box to the org chart.

4. In the assistant box, type *Redmond BEAT*.

5. Add two subordinate boxes to Washington BEAT by clicking the Washington BEAT box to select it, clicking the Subordinate button on the Org Chart toolbar twice (note that the status bar displays *Create: 2*), moving the mouse pointer (which is now shaped like a subordinate box) to the Washington BEAT box, and clicking once.

6. In the new subordinate boxes, type *Vancouver BEAT* and *Spokane BEAT*, respectively.

7. Repeat step 5 to add two subordinate boxes to Oregon BEAT.

8. In the new subordinate boxes, type *Salem BEAT* and *Medford BEAT*, respectively. (Use the scroll bars to scroll the boxes into view, if necessary.)

9. Remove the "empty" box next to Oregon BEAT by selecting it and pressing Delete. The org chart now looks like the one shown on the next page.

Deleting boxes

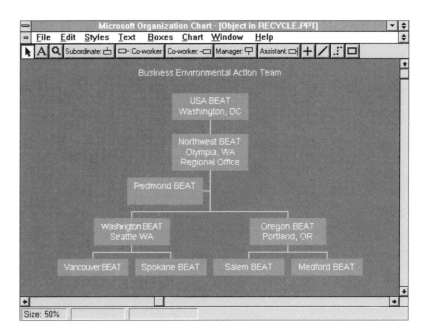

Rearranging Boxes

If you're not happy with the present arrangement of boxes in your org chart, you can use the mouse to rearrange them in a variety of ways. For example, you can promote a subordinate box to a coworker position or demote a manager box to a subordinate position. You can also simply shift boxes to the left or right. Follow these steps to rearrange some of the boxes in the sample org chart:

1. Point to the Oregon BEAT box, hold down the left mouse button, and then drag the box's frame over the Washington BEAT box.

2. When the pointer changes to a left-pointing arrow, release the mouse button. The Washington BEAT and Oregon BEAT boxes switch places. (Notice that the subordinate boxes below Oregon BEAT have moved as well.)

As you've seen, you can determine a box's new position by keeping an eye on the shape of the mouse pointer. A left-pointing arrow indicates that the box will appear to the left of the existing box; a right-pointing arrow indicates that the box will appear to the right of the existing box; and a subordinate box indicates that the box will appear below the existing box. Try the following:

Changing org chart defaults

Use the Options command on Microsoft Organization Chart's Edit menu to change the default settings for org charts. The 4-Box Template option (the default setting) displays the org chart template with four boxes every time you open a new org chart. The 1-Box Template option displays the org chart template with one box, and the Topmost Box option displays the org chart template with one box and the formatting of the org chart that was active when you selected the option. If you want Org Chart to use the same magnification every time you open a new org chart, select the Current Magnification option (see page 87 for more information about magnification).

1. Point to the Redmond BEAT box, hold down the left mouse button, and drag the box's frame over the bottom half of the Washington BEAT box.

Changing to a lower level

2. When the pointer changes to a subordinate box, release the mouse button.

3. Now deselect the Redmond BEAT box, and using the techniques you've just learned, move the box to the left of the Vancouver BEAT box. After all that reshuffling, here are the results:

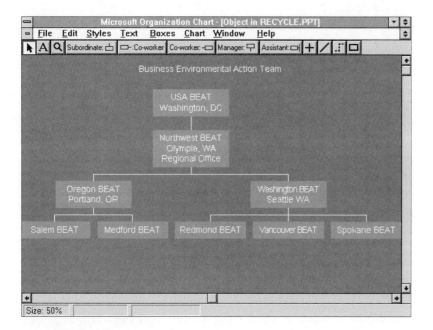

Switching Styles

Before we get into a discussion about styles, you need to familiarize yourself with some terminology. In Org Chart jargon, a *group* refers to the subordinates under a manager, and a *branch* refers to a manager plus all its subordinates. By default, groups are placed side by side in boxes, as in the sample org chart; however, the Org Chart program offers several style alternatives for both groups and branches. For example, you can remove the boxes and display the members of a group or branch vertically, one on top of the other. Or you can convert specific subordinates to assistants or comanagers with the Assistants or Co-Managers style.

Org chart size

When you create an org chart for a PowerPoint presentation, remember to maintain a reasonable size for the org chart. If your org chart is too small, viewers may not be able to read the contents of the org chart boxes. In addition, if your org chart contains several boxes, you might consider breaking the org chart up and placing it on separate slides so that viewers aren't overwhelmed with information.

Selecting groups and branches

To change the style of a group or branch, you must first select it. To select a group, you can select one member of the group and then press Ctrl+G; you can choose Select and then Group from Org Chart's Edit menu; or you can use the selection tool on the Org Chart toolbar to draw a selection box around the group. To select a branch, you can select one member of the branch and then press Ctrl+B; you can choose Select and then Branch from Org Chart's Edit menu; or you can use the selection tool to draw a selection box around the branch.

Experiment with some of the other org chart styles by following these steps:

1. Select the Redmond BEAT box, and press Ctrl+G. All three Washington BEAT subordinate boxes are now selected.

2. From Org Chart's Styles menu, choose the second style in the first row. The org chart looks like this:

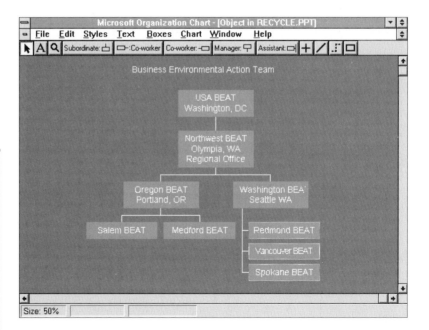

3. Now point above and to the left of the Salem BEAT box with the arrow pointer (aka the *selection tool*), hold down the left mouse button, and drag a selection box around the two subordinates under Oregon BEAT. (In order to select the subordinate boxes using this method, you must completely enclose the boxes in the selection box.)

Selecting specific levels

In addition to the Select commands on Org Chart's Edit menu, you can use the Select Levels command to select all the boxes at a specified level in your org chart. When you choose the Select Levels command from the Edit menu, Org Chart displays the Select Levels dialog box, in which you enter the org chart levels you want to select. For example, if your org chart has 4 levels and you want to select levels 1 through 3, enter *1* in the first edit box, *3* in the second edit box, and click OK.

4. If two or more members of an organization share the same manager as well as the same responsibilities, those members can be designated as comanagers. To designate the selected boxes as comanagers, choose the Co-manager style from Org Chart's Styles menu by clicking its icon.

Designating comanagers

Now condense the org chart by changing the style of its main branch:

1. With any box selected, choose Select and then All from Org Chart's Edit menu.

Condensing the org chart

2. From Org Chart's Styles menu, choose the third style in the first row. Here are the results:

Formatting the Org Chart

You can format the text, boxes, and lines in an org chart by using the commands on Org Chart's Text and Boxes menus. The following sections discuss each of these components in turn and how you can spruce them up with a bit of formatting here and there.

Formatting Org Chart Text

If you pull down Org Chart's Text menu, you'll see commands that allow you to change the font, color, and alignment of the text in an org chart. We won't go into detail about

Magnifying an org chart

You can use the commands on Org Chart's Chart menu to adjust the magnification of an org chart. The following list describes each command:

- Size To Window displays the entire org chart in the Org Chart window.
- 50% Of Actual displays the org chart at 50% of Actual Size.
- Actual Size displays the org chart at approximately 50% larger than its printed size.
- 200% Of Actual displays the org chart at 200% of Actual Size.

You can also use the Enlarge button on the Org Chart toolbar (the button with the magnifying glass icon) to zoom in on areas of the org chart. After you click the Enlarge button, the Reduce button (the button with the org chart icon) appears in its place so that you can zoom out. (The Reduce button has the same effect as the Size To Window command.)

the alignment commands—Left, Right, and Center (the default)—because they are self-explanatory. However, you can follow the steps below to change the font size and color of the text in the chart title so that the *BEAT* in *Business Environmental Action Team* really stands out. Keep in mind that you can use these same techniques to change the text in the org chart boxes too.

Changing the font

1. With the sample org chart displayed in the Org Chart window, select the entire chart title.

2. Choose Font from Org Chart's Text menu, and when the Font dialog box appears, select 28 in the Size list, and click OK.

3. Next, select the *B* in *Business*, choose Font from Org Chart's Text menu, and when the Font dialog box appears, select Bold in the Font Style list, 36 in the Size list, and click OK.

4. With the *B* in *Business* still selected, choose Color from Org Chart's Text menu, and then select yellow in the Color drop-down list.

5. Repeat steps 3 and 4 for the first letter in each of the remaining words of the chart title—*Environmental*, *Action*, and *Team*.

Formatting Org Chart Boxes

On page 81, we showed you how to change the interior color of the org chart boxes using the Box Color command on Org Chart's Boxes menu. Let's now take a look at the other two Box commands: Box Border and Box Shadow:

1. Press Ctrl+A to select all the boxes in the org chart, and choose Box Border from Org Chart's Boxes menu to display this list of border options:

Background color

To quickly change an org chart's background color, choose the Background Color command from the Chart menu, and select a color from the drop-down list of colors.

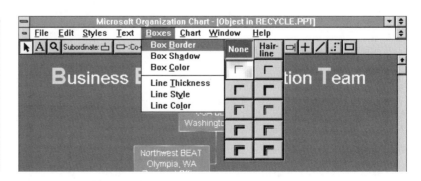

2. Select the fourth border option in the second column.

3. Next, choose Box Shadow from Org Chart's Boxes menu to display this list of shadow options:

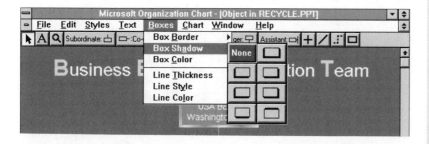

4. Select the second shadow option in the second column.

At this point, you may be wondering why the heck you added a border and a shadow when you can't see them clearly against the black interior color of the org chart boxes. Well, read on.

Formatting Org Chart Lines

You can use the three Line commands on Org Chart's Boxes menu to change the thickness, style, and color of the connecting lines in an org chart. Obviously, before you can change the lines, you must select them. To select a single connecting line, simply click it with the mouse. To select multiple lines, hold down the Shift key as you click each line, or choose Select and then Connecting Lines from Org Chart's Edit menu. (If you happen to select org chart boxes as well as lines when using the first method, any changes you make using the Line commands also affects the borders of the boxes.)

1. Choose Select and then Connecting Lines from Org Chart's Edit menu. (You know a line has been selected when it turns light gray.)

2. Choose Line Thickness from Org Chart's Boxes menu, and select the 3 Pt line option to increase the thickness of the connecting lines.

3. With all the lines still selected, choose Line Style from Org Chart's Boxes menu, and select the Dashed line option.

4. Click anywhere outside the Org Chart to deselect the connecting lines, press Ctrl+A, choose Line Color from Org Chart's

Drawing lines and boxes

At the right end of the Org Chart toolbar, you'll find four drawing tools. (If you don't see the tools, choose the Show Draw Tools command from Org Chart's Chart menu.) If Org Chart's built-in box arrangements don't quite satisfy your requirements, you can use these tools to draw lines and boxes exactly where they're needed. For example, the first two tools allow you to draw perpendicular and diagonal lines, respectively. The third tool lets you draw connecting lines, and the fourth tool lets you draw boxes. To use a drawing tool, click it, position the mouse pointer at the starting point for the line or box, hold down the left mouse button, and drag to the ending point for the line or box. (When you use the Connecting Line tool, you must be sure to drag from the edge of the first box to the edge of the second box.) You can resize a line or box by dragging its handles, and you can reposition a line or box by placing the mouse pointer on the line or box border, holding down the left mouse button, and dragging to a new location on the org chart. By the way, lines and boxes created with the drawing tools are actually part of the org chart's background, so they remain stationary when you move or resize the org chart. As a result, you should finalize any adjustments to the org chart before you draw lines or boxes.

Boxes menu, and select yellow from the drop-down list of colors. The results are shown below (sans color, of course):

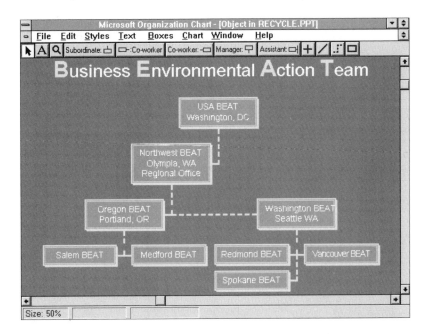

Note that because you selected the boxes as well as the lines in step 4 (by pressing Ctrl+A), the yellow Line Color option was applied to the borders of the org chart boxes as well. Now the borders and shadows you added in the previous section stand out much better.

Returning to PowerPoint

After your org chart is complete, quitting Org Chart and returning to PowerPoint automatically adds the org chart to the current slide. Once the org chart is in place, you can use the mouse to reposition or resize it. (You can return to the Org Chart program at any time by double-clicking the org chart on the slide.) Follow these steps to return to PowerPoint:

Quitting Microsoft Organization Chart

1. Choose Update RECYCLE.PPT from Org Chart's File menu. (If you don't choose this command first, you will be prompted to update the org chart before proceeding.)

2. Choose the Exit And Return To RECYCLE.PPT command from Org Chart's File menu.

Back in PowerPoint, several adjustments are in order. First, you need to remove the slide's title placeholder because the org chart comes equipped with a title. Second, you need to resize the org chart to fill the current slide. Follow these steps:

1. Click the title area of the slide, press F2 until the title placeholder is surrounded by handles, and then press Delete to remove the placeholder.

Deleting the title placeholder

2. Click the object area once to select the org chart, point to the top center handle, and when the pointer changes to a double-headed arrow, drag upward a couple of inches. You can turn on the rulers if you need guidance (see page 37).

Sizing the org chart

3. Use the side handles to widen the org chart about 1/2 inch on both sides. Here are the final results:

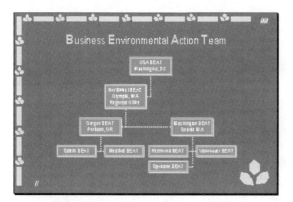

Creating Tables

Adding tables to PowerPoint slides is a snap as long as you also have Microsoft Word 6 for Windows. Unlike graphs and org charts, whose program modules are included with Power-Point, tables can be created only by borrowing Word's table-making capabilities (or by importing tables from another application, which is a topic beyond the scope of this book). If you purchased PowerPoint as part of the Microsoft Office package, you'll have no problem; Word 6 is part of that package too. If you don't have Word 6 and you plan to create tables for your presentations, it's a good idea to get yourself over to the nearest software store and pick up a copy. (While you're at it, you'll also need a copy of *A Quick Course in Word 6 for Windows* so that you can bone up on Word!)

Adding a table to an existing slide

If you want to add a table to an existing slide, rather than create a brand new table slide, move to the desired slide, click the Insert Microsoft Word Table button on the Standard toolbar, and when the drop-down table grid appears, drag across the number of columns (up to 13) and down the number of rows (up to 5) you want in the table. You can also choose the Microsoft Word Table command from the Insert menu, and enter the number of columns and rows in the Insert Word Table dialog box.

In the following sections, we'll show you how to add a table to a slide, enter data, modify the table's structure, and format the table. We've got a lot to do, so let's get started:

1. With the RECYCLE.PPT presentation open in Slide view, move to Slide 5.

2. Click the New Slide button at the bottom of the Presentation window, and when the New Slide dialog box appears, double-click the Table AutoLayout (the third AutoLayout in the third row of the AutoLayout list).

3. Double-click the table placeholder in the object area of the new slide to display this dialog box:

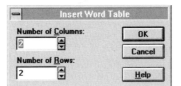

Specifying the number of columns and rows

4. Type *4* in the Number Of Columns edit box, double-click the Number Of Rows edit box, type *5*, and click OK. Word 6's menu bar and toolbars have replaced those of PowerPoint, and an empty table surrounded by a gray frame and containing the number of columns and rows you specified appears:

Word's menu bar

Word's Standard toolbar

Word's Formatting toolbar

Table

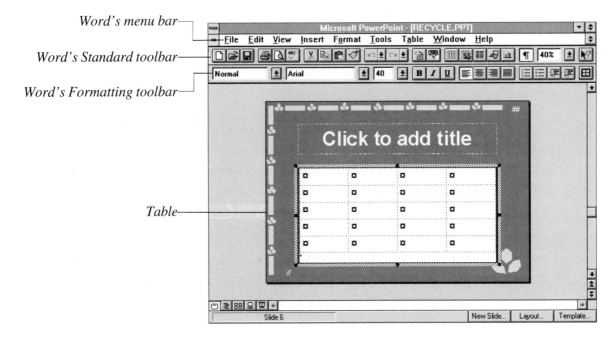

Like the datasheet in Graph, the table is divided into units called *cells*. The gridlines that demarcate the cells can be turned on and off by choosing Gridlines from Word's Table menu. (These gridlines, by the way, do not appear on the actual PowerPoint slide.) An insertion point rests in the first cell of the table, just to the left of a circular end-of-cell marker. You'll find similar end-of-row markers at the end of each row in the table.

Table cells

5. If rulers appear across the top and down the left side of the table, choose Ruler from the View menu to turn them off. (You don't need the rulers right now.)

Entering Data

You enter data in a table the same way you enter data elsewhere in PowerPoint, by simply typing. When you enter data, it is entered at the location of the insertion point. You can move the insertion point to another cell by clicking the cell with the mouse or by using the key and key combinations listed below:

Moving the insertion point

Key(s)	Moves insertion point
Up or Down Arrow	Up or down one line or cell
Left or Right Arrow	Left or right one character or cell
Tab	To next cell
Shift+Tab	To previous cell
Alt+Home	To first cell in current row
Alt+End	To last cell in current row
Alt+PageUp	To first cell in current column
Alt+PageDown	To last cell in current column

If you make a mistake, use the Backspace or Delete key; and if you want to start a new paragraph within a cell, use the Enter key. Try the following:

1. With the insertion point located in the first cell of the table, type *Brand*, and press Tab. Type *Post-Consumer Waste*, press Tab, and type *Recycled*.

Entering headings

The font size is too large for a table. Looking at Word's Formatting toolbar, you can see that the font and font size, Arial 40, have been carried over to the table from the

Table math

The Formula command on Word's Table menu allows you to perform mathematical calculations on the data in your tables. For the Formula command to work, each cell in the table is assigned an address consisting of the cell's column letter and row number. The first cell is A1, the cell below A1 is A2, the cell to the right of A1 is B1, and so on. To enter a formula, click an insertion point in the cell where you want the results field to appear, and then choose Formula from the Table menu. Word displays the Formula dialog box, in which you enter the formula you want to use in your calculation. By default, if you place the insertion point in a cell below a column of numbers, then choose the Formula command, and click OK in the Formula dialog box, Word enters =SUM(ABOVE) in the selected cell and sums the numbers in the column. To sum the numbers in a row, change the formula to =SUM(RIGHT) or =SUM(LEFT), depending on the location of the insertion point. To use a function other than SUM, delete all but the equal sign in the Formula edit box, select a function from the Paste Function drop-down list, and enter the appropriate cells or cell range in the function's parentheses. (When you enter two or more cells, the cells must be separated with a comma, as in A1,D1. When you enter a cell range, the cells must be separated with a colon, as in A1:D1.)

TREES.PPT template. To decrease the font size for the entire table, follow these steps:

1. With the insertion point located anywhere in the table, choose Select Table from Word's Table menu. The entire table is highlighted.

2. Double-click the Font Size box on Word's Formatting toolbar, type *30*, and press Enter.

Now continue entering data in the table:

1. In the second cell of the first column, type *Hammermill*, press Tab, type *50%*, press Tab again, and type *100%*.

2. Using the navigation techniques listed on the previous page, complete the table in RECYCLE.PPT with this information:

Cross-Pointe	100%	100%
Graphika	60%	100%
Eureka!	25%	50%

3. So that you can see all the data, drag the handles around the table's frame until the table completely fills the slide, like this:

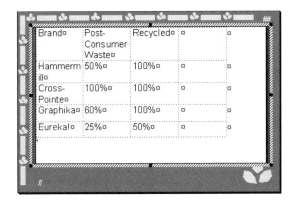

4. To save the table, return to PowerPoint by clicking anywhere outside the table, and then click the Save button on the Standard toolbar.

5. To continue working on the table, double-click the table on the PowerPoint slide.

Inserting and Deleting Columns and Rows

The Insert and Delete commands at the top of Word's Table menu change to reflect whatever table component is currently selected. If a column is selected, you'll see Insert Columns and Delete Columns at the top of Word's Table menu. If a row is selected, you'll see Insert Rows and Delete Rows. If a cell is selected, the commands change to Insert Cells and Delete Cells (see the tip at the bottom of the page).

Before you can insert or delete a column or row, you must make a selection so that Word knows where you want the insertion or deletion to take place. To select a column, drag through the cells of the column, or click any cell in the column and choose Select Column from Word's Table menu. To select a row, drag through the cells of the row (be sure to include the end-of-row marker), or click any cell in the row and choose Select Row from Word's Table menu. If you select multiple columns or rows before choosing the Insert or Delete command, Word inserts or deletes that many columns or rows.

Selecting columns and rows

Let's insert a new column to the left of the Recycled column in the sample table:

1. With the table displayed in Word, click any cell in the Recycled column, and choose Select Column from Word's Table menu.

2. Choose Insert Columns from Word's Table menu.

3. In the first cell of the new column, type *Deinked* as the column heading. (You'll fill in the remaining cells later.)

If you make a mistake when inserting or deleting columns or rows, click the Undo button or use the Undo command on Word's Edit menu.

Now insert a new row at the top of the table:

1. Click any cell in the first row, and choose Select Row from Word's Table menu.

2. Choose Insert Rows from Word's Table menu.

Inserting and deleting cells

When you select a cell or cells in a table without selecting an entire column or row, the commands at the top of Word's Table menu become Insert Cells and Delete Cells. Depending on which command you choose, Word displays the Insert Cells or Delete Cells dialog box. You can then specify how the remaining cells should move after the insertion or deletion and whether an entire row or column should be inserted or deleted.

3. In the first cell of the new row, type *Post-Consumer Office Paper.*

Deleting rows and columns is as simple as inserting them. Follow these steps:

Deleting columns

1. Select the last column in the table.

2. Choose Delete Columns from the Table menu.

Moving and Copying Columns and Rows

Using drag-and-drop techniques, you can move or copy columns and rows in a table. After you select a column or row, simply drag it between two other columns or rows to move it. Or hold down the Ctrl key as you drag to copy rather than move the column or row. You can move or copy multiple columns or rows by selecting them all before you drag.

Keep in mind that when you move or copy a row, you must first select the entire row, including the end-of-row marker; otherwise, the contents of the destination row will be over-written by the contents of the moved or copied row.

Try moving the Recycled column to the right of the Brand column:

1. With the table displayed in Word, select the Recycled column.

Quick-selection techniques

To quickly select a column in a table, place the mouse pointer at the top of the column, and when the pointer changes to a down arrow, click the left mouse button to select the entire column. To quickly select a row, place the mouse pointer to the left of the row, and when the pointer changes to a right-pointing arrow, double-click to select the entire row, including the end-of-row marker.

2. Point to the column, hold down the left mouse button, drag the shadow insertion point to the second column in the table, and release the mouse button to drop the column into place.

Moving and Copying Cells

In addition to using drag-and-drop techniques, you can use the Cut, Copy, and Paste buttons on Word's Standard toolbar or the Cut, Copy, and Paste commands on Word's Edit menu to move or copy the contents of a cell. (You can also use the Cut, Copy, and Paste commands on the shortcut menu that appears when you click a selected cell with the right mouse button.)

Like end-of-row markers, end-of-cell markers play an important part in determining how the contents of a cell are moved or copied. If you include the end-of-cell marker in your selection, the contents of the moved or copied cell overwrite the contents of the destination cell. If you don't include the end-of-cell marker, the contents of the moved or copied cell are added to the contents of the destination cell.

Practice copying cells by following these steps:

1. Click the first blank cell below the Deinked column heading, and type *Yes*.

2. Next, triple-click the cell to select both its contents and end-of-cell marker, and click the Copy button on the Standard toolbar.

3. Click the blank cell below the selected cell, and then click the Paste button on the Standard toolbar.

4. Repeat step 3 for the last cell in the Deinked column.

5. Finally, in the remaining blank cell, type *No*.

Copying cells

Adjusting Column Width and Row Height

The fastest way to adjust column widths and row heights in a table is to adjust the dotted gridlines between the columns and rows or to adjust the column and row markers on the rulers. For example, to decrease the width of a column, you can drag the gridline that runs along the column's right side to the left. Or, to increase the height of a row, you can drag the row marker that aligns with the bottom of the row down.

Adjust the widths of the columns in the sample table by following these steps:

1. Choose Ruler from Word's View menu to turn on the horizontal and vertical rulers. The rulers run along the top and left side of the table, and a tab alignment button, currently displaying the symbol for left-aligned tabs, sits at the intersection of the rulers. You can change the tab-alignment setting from left to center to right to decimal by simply clicking this button.

Tab alignment button

2. Point to the gridline to the right of the Brand column, and when the pointer changes to a double bar with arrows, hold

Manually adjusting column width

down the left mouse button and drag to the 2 3/4-inch position on the horizontal ruler.

3. Repeat step 2, moving the right border of the Recycled column to the 5-inch position on the horizontal ruler.

4. Next, point to the column marker that designates the right border of the Post-Consumer Waste column on the ruler, and when the pointer changes to a double-headed arrow, hold down the left mouse button, and drag the marker to the 71/4-inch position on the horizontal ruler.

If you want a more precise way to set column widths and row heights or if you want to change the widths and heights of multiple columns and rows simultaneously, you can use the Cell Height And Width command on Word's Table menu, like this:

Using the Cell Height And Width command

1. Click anywhere in the Deinked column, and choose Select Column from Word's Table menu.

2. Choose Cell Height And Width from Word's Table menu to display the Cell Height And Width dialog box shown below:

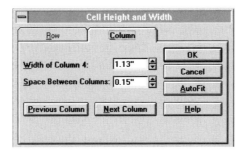

In this dialog box, you can specify row heights and column widths, as well as a number of other settings. On the Column tab, you can specify the width of the selected columns, as well

Sizing column width to longest entry

as the space between columns. Or, you can click the AutoFit button to set the width of each selected column to the width of the longest entry in each column. You can click the Previous Column or Next Column button to quickly move to other columns in the table. On the Row tab, you can select

Setting row height

from three options in the Height Of Row drop-down list: Auto adjusts the row height to the height of the tallest cell in the row; At Least adjusts the height to a minimum setting (specified by you in the adjacent At edit box); and Exactly adjusts the height to an exact setting (specified by you in the At edit box). You can also specify indent and alignment settings for the text in the selected rows and indicate whether the rows can break across a page.

Setting indents and alignment

3. On the Column tab, double-click the Width Of Column 4 edit box, type *2*, and then click OK. The table now looks like this:

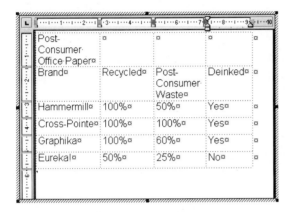

Merging and Splitting Cells

To include headings that span more than one column in a table, you can convert two or more cells to one large cell by using the Merge Cells command on Word's Table menu. To create a heading for the sample table, let's merge the cells in the first row:

1. Select all four cells in the first row of the table.

Creating headings that span columns

2. Choose Merge Cells from Word's Table menu. Here is the result:

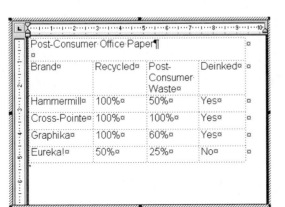

If you choose Merge Cells by mistake, you can click the Undo button to return the merged cells to their original state. If you decide later that you don't want the cells to be merged, you

Splitting merged cells → can choose Split Cells from Word's Table menu. Word then displays the Split Cells dialog box, in which you specify the number of columns you want to split the selected cell into.

Sorting the Data

You can sort the data in a table by using the Sort command on Word's Table menu. Here's how to sort the brand names in the first column of the sample table:

1. Turn off the rulers by choosing Ruler from Word's View menu.

2. Select the four brand names in the first column (Hammermill, Cross-Pointe, Graphika, and Eureka!).

3. Choose Sort from Word's Table menu to display the dialog box shown here:

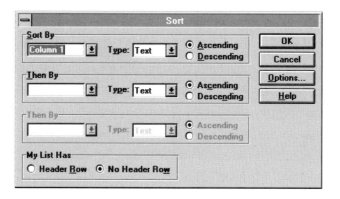

Specifying sort options → In the Sort dialog box, you can specify the column you want to sort by, the type of sort you want to perform (text, number, or date), and the order of the sort (ascending or descending). If you don't want to include the first row of the selected column in the sort because it contains a header, you can select the Header Row option at the bottom of the dialog box.

4. Accept the default settings by clicking OK. Here are the results:

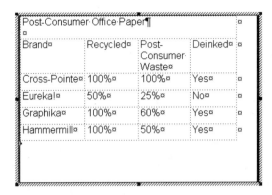

Post-Consumer Office Paper¶				¤
¤				
Brand¤	Recycled¤	Post-Consumer Waste¤	Deinked¤	¤
Cross-Pointe¤	100%¤	100%¤	Yes¤	¤
Eureka!¤	50%¤	25%¤	No¤	¤
Graphika¤	100%¤	60%¤	Yes¤	¤
Hammermill¤	100%¤	50%¤	Yes¤	¤

Note that Word not only sorts the data in the selected column but also sorts the corresponding data in the adjacent columns.

Formatting the Table

In addition to formatting the table's data, you can also format the table as a whole by adding a border and shading. In this section, we'll try our hands at both types of formatting.

Formatting the Data

Because PowerPoint and Word are so closely related, the techniques for formatting data in Word are very similar to those in PowerPoint. In fact, the Formatting toolbars of both programs share many of the same buttons. As with Power-Point, you can also use commands on Word's Format and shortcut menus to format the table's data. Follow these steps to format the data in the sample table:

1. With the table in RECYCLE.PPT displayed in Word, select the table heading in the first row by triple-clicking it, and choose Font from Word's Format menu.

2. On the Font tab of the Font dialog box, select Bold in the Font Style list, select 36 in the Size list, and then click OK.

3. Next, select the entire row of column headings below the table heading, and click the Bold button on the Formatting toolbar. The results are shown on the next page.

Table AutoFormats

When you choose Table Auto-Format from Word's Table menu, the Table AutoFormat dialog box appears. You can then select from a list of predefined table formats with borders, shading, special fonts, and so on already built in. The format you select is displayed in the Preview box. Select or de-select options in the Formats To Apply and Apply Special Formats To sections to tailor the Auto-Format to suit your needs.

Adding a Border and Shading

If you want to dress up your table a bit or call attention to specific information in the table, you can add borders and/or shading using the Borders And Shading command on Word's Format menu. Try the following:

1. With the sample table displayed in Word and the insertion point located anywhere in the table, choose Borders And Shading from Word's Format menu to display this dialog box:

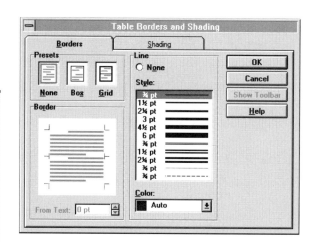

Borders toolbar

In addition to the Borders And Shading command on Word's Format menu, you can use Word's Borders toolbar to add borders to your table. Just click the Borders button at the right end of Word's Formatting toolbar to display the Borders toolbar. Then select the table or the section of the table you want to add a border to, and click the appropriate button(s) on the toolbar. You can even change the border style with the Line Style box and add shading with the Shading box. If you want to remove borders, use the No Borders button.

2. In the Presets section of the Borders tab, select Grid to add a border and gridlines to the table. (To add just a border to the table, you would select the Box option.)

3. In the Line section, select 3 Pt from the Style list and Yellow from the Color drop-down list, and click OK to close the dialog box.

4. Next, select the first row of the table (the row containing the table heading), and then choose Borders And Shading from

Word's Format menu. (When you select a single row, the Table Borders And Shading dialog box becomes the Cell Borders And Shading dialog box.)

5. Click the Shading tab, and select 25% in the Shading list. (If you want, you can change the foreground and background colors of the shaded area using the appropriate drop-down lists on the Shading tab.)

6. Click OK to close the dialog box. Here's what the table looks like now:

Post-Consumer·Office·Paper¶				¤
¤				
Brand¤	Recycled¤	Post-Consumer· Waste¤	Deinked¤	¤
Cross-Pointe¤	100%¤	100%¤	Yes¤	¤
Eurekal¤	50%¤	25%¤	No¤	¤
Graphika¤	100%¤	60%¤	Yes¤	¤
Hammermill¤	100%¤	50%¤	Yes¤	¤

Finishing Up

After all that work, you're ready to return to PowerPoint. Like the graphs and org chart you added earlier, the table will need a few adjustments on the slide. Follow these steps to make those adjustments now:

1. Click anywhere outside the table to return to PowerPoint.

2. Move the table down until you can see the slide's empty title placeholder. This placeholder will not appear when the slide is printed or displayed in Slide Show view, but you might find its presence annoying in other views, so click it, then click its frame to select it, and press the Delete key.

3. Click the table to select it, and drag the table into position on the slide, using the dotted placeholder as a guide.

4. If the table bumps into other elements on the slide, reduce its size by dragging its handles.

To see what the finished product looks like, turn to page 79 and check out Slide 6.

Putting on the Glitz:
Adding Graphics

On Slide 3 of REDBEAT1.PPT, we added a graphic from the ClipArt Gallery and changed its color. On Slide 1, we added a background graphic and cropped it to simulate splitting. We inserted a Paintbrush graphic on Slide 5. And finally, we used the drawing tools to highlight the speaker's name on Slide 1.

Toward a Healthy
Environment

Ted Lee

Redmond Business Environmental Action Team

Vision Statement

- By the year 2000, all Redmond companies will have evaluated their business practices and implemented any changes necessary to promote a healthy environment

---

Goals

- Increase business awareness
- Encourage win-win solutions
- Stop waste
- Reduce the nation's garbage bill

Rationale

- If we don't do it ourselves, government will do it for us

Today's Situation

- 56 members out of 432 businesses
- 10 new members a month
- 5 Business Ambassadors
- 2 Pinnacle Sponsors
  - » GlassWorks
  - » EarthWare

How Did We Get Here?

- Chartered as a chapter of USA BEAT in 1989
- Originally staffed by volunteers
- Offices rented and a full-time coordinator hired in 1992
- First annual Achievement Awards in 1993

Activities

- Publish On the BEAT newsletter and online forum
- Maintain resource center
- Conduct on-site analyses
- Support local recycling efforts
- Community outreach

Join Us!

- Grass-roots effort
- Successful track record
- Strength in numbers

ClipArt Gallery

E ven if you are not an artist, PowerPoint's ClipArt Gallery and drawing tools can make you look like one. You can use the pictures in the ClipArt Gallery to dress up your presentation's slides, and with hundreds of pictures to choose from, the ClipArt Gallery has a picture to fit just about any need. If, by chance, you can't find the right piece of clip art, or if you're on the creative side, you can use the tools on PowerPoint's Drawing toolbars to produce your own masterpieces, which you can then add to your presentation's slides.

This chapter focuses on some of the ways you can enrich slides with ready-made art or drawings you create yourself. We show you how to add clip art graphics to slides and how to size and manipulate the graphics. We also discuss importing graphics from other sources into your PowerPoint presentations. And we show you how to add new graphics to the ClipArt Gallery so that they're always at your fingertips. Finally, we introduce you to PowerPoint's drawing tools and give you some pointers for creating your own artwork. Before we get started, however, you might want to read the adjacent tip to be sure all of PowerPoint's clip art graphics are installed on your system.

Installing all the Clip Art files

If you performed a Typical Installation (the default) rather than a Complete Installation when you installed PowerPoint, you won't have all of Power-Point's clip art graphics available. To remedy the situation, run PowerPoint's Setup program, and when the Setup dialog box appears, click the Add/Remove button to display the Maintenance Mode dialog box. Use the Down Arrow key to highlight the Clip Art Files option in the Options list (don't deselect its check box), and click the Change Option button. In the Clip Art Files dialog box, select all the options (or as many as you have space for—check the information at the bottom of the dialog box) in the Options list, and then click OK. When you return to the Maintenance Mode dialog box, click Continue. Setup then guides you through the rest of the procedure, instructing you to insert disks and so on.

Adding Clip Art to Slides

You can add clip art to existing slides or select the clip art AutoLayouts in the New Slide dialog box to create brand new slides with clip art placeholders. Using the REDBEAT1.PPT presentation you created in Chapter 1, we'll show you how to add clip art to an existing slide. (For information about creating new slides with clip art, see the tip on page 107.)

1. Open REDBEAT1.PPT, and display Slide 3 in Slide view.

2. Click the Insert Clip Art button on the Standard toolbar or choose the Clip Art command from the Insert menu. If this is the first time you've used the ClipArt Gallery, you'll see the Add Clipart dialog box, informing you that ClipArt Gallery is adding pictures. This procedure may take a few minutes, but it's a onetime occurrence. The next time you insert clip

art, you won't have to wait for the Gallery to add pictures. Then this dialog box appears:

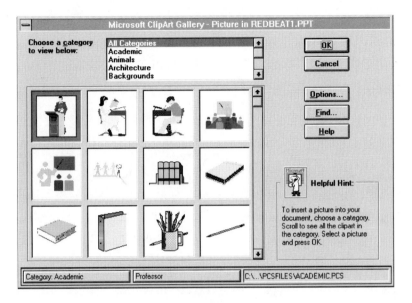

3. Scroll the categories list, and select the Household category.

Selecting a category

4. Next, scroll the ClipArt Gallery until you see the garbage can graphic, and click the graphic to select it. PowerPoint surrounds the graphic with a heavy border.

5. Click OK to insert the graphic on Slide 3. (You can also simply double-click the graphic.) Here are the results:

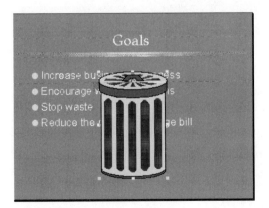

6. Choose Save As from the File menu, save the presentation as REDBEAT2.PPT, and click OK to close the Summary Info dialog box without entering any information. (As usual, we won't tell you to save from here on out, but you should remember to save often.)

New clip art slides

If you want to create a brand new clip art slide, rather than add a clip art graphic to an existing slide, simply click the New Slide button at the bottom of the Presentation window, and then select one of the clip art AutoLayouts in the New Slide dialog box.

Resizing and Repositioning Clip Art

Like other objects in PowerPoint, you can easily resize and relocate clip art graphics on a slide. Follow these simple steps to change the size and location of the garbage can graphic:

1. If the garbage can graphic is not currently selected (surrounded with handles), click it once to select it.

Sizing graphics

2. Point to one of the graphic's top corner handles, and when the pointer changes to a double-headed arrow, hold down the left mouse button, and drag down about 2 inches. (If necessary, choose Ruler from the View menu, and use the rulers as a guide.) Dragging a corner handle, rather than a side handle, changes the height and width of the graphic proportionally. You can use this technique to change the height and width of any object in PowerPoint.

Moving graphics

3. Position the mouse pointer over the graphic, hold down the left mouse button, and drag to the right about 3 inches.

4. Click anywhere outside the graphic to deselect it. Slide 3 now looks like this:

Scaling bitmapped graphics

When you add a bitmapped graphic, such as a scanned photograph, to a slide, you can resize the graphic like any other object by dragging its handles. After you resize a bitmapped graphic, you can easily return it to its original proportions by choosing the Scale command from the Draw menu and selecting the Relative To Original Picture Size option in the Scale dialog box. To enlarge or reduce the graphic, change the percentage in the Scale To edit box. (You can drag the Scale dialog box out of the way and click the Preview button to see the results.)

Recoloring Clip Art

You aren't restricted to the predefined set of colors assigned to a clip art graphic. You can use the options in the Recolor Picture dialog box to change any color in the graphic. Try your hand at recoloring the garbage can graphic now:

1. Select the graphic, and choose Recolor from the Tools menu to display this dialog box:

If you want to change any and all colors of the clip art graphic, select the Colors option in the Change section of the dialog box. If you're only interested in changing the background or fill colors of the graphic, select the Fills option.

2. Select the third check box in the Original section, open the adjacent drop-down list of colors in the New section, and select the light green color. (By default, the drop-down list presents you with the eight colors of the current color scheme. If you want to use a different color, you can click the Other Color option to display the Other Color dialog box, and then select a color from the Color palette or click the More Colors button to create a custom color; see the tip on page 52 for more information. If you stick with the color scheme colors, however, you're assured that the colors you select for the clip art graphic will coordinate with the other colors on the slide, and, if you change the slide's color scheme, the colors of the graphic will change accordingly.)

Selecting a new color

3. Click the Preview button to see the effects of your recoloring, and then click OK.

Previewing the colors

Searching for Clip Art

When you first opened the Microsoft ClipArt Gallery dialog box, you might have noticed the Find button. Rather than scroll through the hundreds of graphics in the Gallery, you can click the Find button and use the options in the Find Picture dialog box to locate a specific clip art graphic. Find the fir tree graphic and insert it on Slide 1 of REDBEAT2.PPT by following the steps on the next page.

1. With REDBEAT2.PPT on your screen, move to Slide 1.

2. Click the Insert Clip Art button on the Standard toolbar, and when the Microsoft ClipArt Gallery dialog box appears, click the Find button to display the Find Picture dialog box:

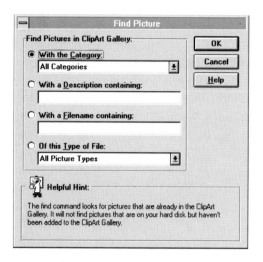

Search parameters

To search by category, select a category from the With The Category list. To search by description, enter a keyword in the With A Description Containing edit box. To search by filename, enter part or all of the clip art file's name in the With A Filename Containing edit box, and to search by file type, select a file type from the Of This Type Of File list.

3. Select the With A Description Containing option, enter *fir* in the edit box, and click OK to display these results:

Replacing clip art

If you change your mind about a clip art graphic you have added to a presentation, you can easily replace it. Just double-click the graphic to open the Microsoft ClipArt Gallery dialog box, and then select a different graphic.

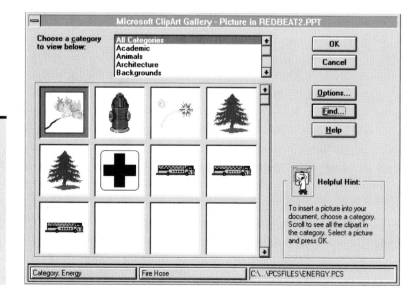

As you can see, any graphic with *fir* as part of its description, such as *fire hose* and *fireworks*, is displayed in the Gallery.

4. Double-click the fir tree graphic to insert it on Slide 1.

If the results of your search don't prove to be fruitful, you can always return to the Find Picture dialog box, and enter a different keyword in the With A Description Containing edit box or use one of the other Find options.

Adding Clip Art to the Background

You can add a clip art graphic to the background of one or all slides in a presentation. We'll show you how to do the former in a moment. To do the latter, you must insert the clip art graphic on the presentation's Slide Master, and then choose Send To Back from the Draw menu. (For more information about the Slide Master, see page 41.) Follow these steps to add the fir tree graphic to the background of Slide 1 only:

Adding to all slides

1. Be sure Slide 1 is displayed in Slide view on your screen.

2. If necessary, select the fir tree graphic, and then choose the Send To Back command from the Draw menu. The text of the slide now overlays the graphic, like this:

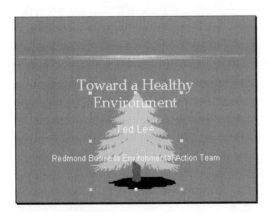

Cropping Clip Art

Just as you can crop a photograph (cut out the part you want to use), you can crop a graphic. Unlike a photograph, however, a cropped graphic can easily be restored to its original condition. Turn the page to see how to crop the fir tree graphic to create a split image like the one on Slide 1 on page 105.

Splitting a graphic in two

1. With the fir tree graphic selected, choose Crop Picture from the Tools menu to activate the cropping tool.

2. Place the cropping tool over the right center handle of the graphic, and drag to the left until the tree is bisected, like this:

3. Click anywhere on the slide to deactivate the cropping tool, and then drag the left half of the fir tree graphic to the right side of the slide, as far as it will go.

Duplicating graphics

4. With the graphic still selected, choose Duplicate from the Edit menu. A second "bisected" tree appears over the first.

5. Add the duplicate tree to Slide 1's background by dragging it to the center of the slide and choosing Send To Back from the Draw menu.

6. Now choose Crop Picture from the Tools menu, and uncrop the graphic.

7. Next, place the cropping tool over the left center handle, and follow the techniques described above to crop the left side of the tree and position it on the left side of Slide 1. To see the results, refer back to page 105.

Importing Graphics from Other Sources

If you want to use a graphic from another application, you'll be happy to know that PowerPoint accepts a multitude of graphics file formats, as long as the proper graphics filters have been installed. (If Microsoft Word or Microsoft Excel is installed on your computer, PowerPoint can share the filters that came with these programs.) Here is a list of the graphics file formats you can import into PowerPoint presentations:

Graphics file format	Extension
AutoCAD Format 2-D	.DXF
AutoCAD Plot File	.ADI
CompuServe GIF	.GIF
Computer Graphics Metafile	.CGM
Corel Draw	.CDR
DrawPerfect	.WPG
Encapsulated PostScript	.EPS
HP Graphic Language	.HGL
HP Plotter Print File	.PLT
Kodak Photo CD	.PCD
Lotus 1-2-3 Graphics	.PIC
Macintosh PICT	.PCT
Micrografx Designer/Draw	.DRW
PC Paintbrush	.PCX
Tagged Image Format	.TIF
Targa	.TGA
Windows Bitmap	.BMP
Windows DIB	.DIB
Windows Metafile	.WMF

Graphics file formats

The procedure for importing graphics into PowerPoint is a snap. To demonstrate just how easy it is to pull a graphic in from another source, we used Paintbrush to create a simple graphic called PINNACLE.BMP, which we will insert on Slide 5 of REDBEAT2.PPT. If you have a graphics file handy, you can follow along now:

1. In Slide view, move to Slide 5, and then choose Picture from the Insert menu to display this dialog box:

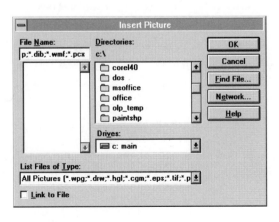

The Find File button

If you have trouble locating a graphics file in the Insert Picture dialog box, click the Find File button, and use the Search option in the Find File dialog box to locate your file. When the Search dialog box appears, you can enter the file's name and/or location to narrow your search. (Be sure the Include Subdirectories option is selected.) You can also click the Advanced Search button in the Search dialog box to search for the file by location, summary information (see page 9), and/or timestamp (the date the file was created or last saved). When the search is complete, the results are displayed in the Find File dialog box. Select the file you want in the Listed Files box, and click the Insert button to insert the contents of the file on the current slide.

2. Select the correct drive from the Drives drop-down list (in this case, C:), and then select the directory where the file is located from the Directories list.

3. Select the name of the graphics file (PINNACLE.BMP, in our case) in the File Name list, and then click OK to insert the graphic on the current slide, like this:

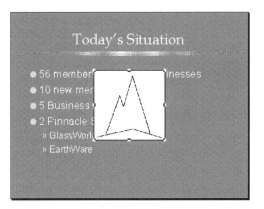

4. Use the mouse to resize the graphic and drag it into position, as we did here:

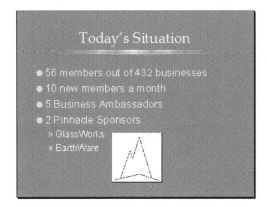

You can also use the same techniques described earlier for clip art to recolor and crop an imported graphic or to add an imported graphic to a slide's background. And, if you have a scanner, you can use the procedure outlined above to import scanned photographs into your PowerPoint presentations too.

Adding Graphics to the ClipArt Gallery

If you want graphics from other applications to be as readily available as the clip art that came with PowerPoint, you can add the graphics to the ClipArt Gallery. Just follow these steps (again, we'll use PINNACLE.BMP as an example):

1. Click the Insert Clip Art button on the Standard toolbar to open the Microsoft ClipArt Gallery dialog box, and then click the Options button to display this dialog box:

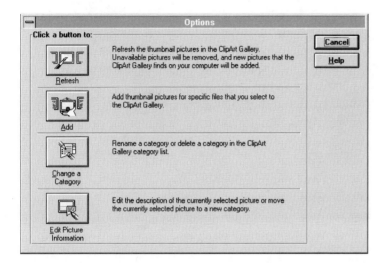

2. Click the Add button to open the first of two Add Clipart dialog boxes:

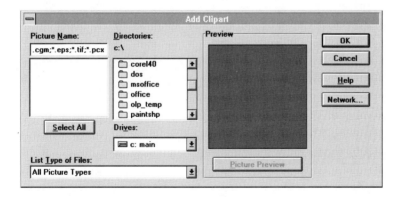

3. Select the type of graphic file you want to add from the List Type Of Files drop down list at the bottom of the dialog box (Windows Bitmap, in our case), and then select the correct drive and directory from the Drives and Directories lists.

4. In the Picture Name list, select the name of the graphics file. (If you want to double-check your selection, click the Picture Preview button.)

Options options

In addition to the Add option in the ClipArt Gallery's Options dialog box, you'll find three other options: Refresh, Change A Category, and Edit Picture Information. Use the Refresh option to update the ClipArt Gallery, removing unavailable graphics and adding new ones. Use the Change A Category option to delete a category in the Gallery. (Note that when you delete a category, the clip art in that category is moved to the All Categories category.) Use the Edit Picture Information option to change the description for the currently selected clip art graphic or to move the graphic to a different category.

5. Click OK to display the second Add Clipart dialog box, where a picture of the current graphic appears in the Preview box:

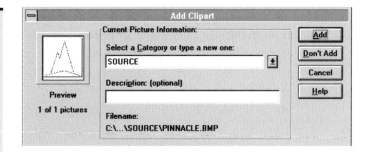

Adding multiple graphics

You can add more than one clip art graphic at a time to the Clip-Art Gallery. First click the Options button in the Microsoft ClipArt Gallery dialog box, and select the Add option. Then, in the first Add Clipart dialog box, select the type of files you want to add in the List Type Of Files drop-down list, and use the Drives and Directories lists to navigate to the files. In the Picture Name list, select all the files by clicking the Select All button, or select specific files by holding down the Ctrl key as you click each file's name. Then click OK to display the second Add Clipart dialog box. Select one of the options in the Categorize Your Clipart section, and click OK. If you choose not to categorize your clip art in this dialog box, all of your selections are added to the Gallery. If you choose to cat-egorize your clip art, a third Add Clipart dialog box appears, in which you can enter category names and descriptions for your selections and then click the Add button to add them to the Gallery. If you decide not to add a partic-ular graphic to the Gallery, you can click the Don't Add button instead. (Note that a preview of each graphic is displayed on the left side of the dialog box, along with a count of the graphics to be added.)

6. Select a category name or type a new one in the first edit box. (We entered the name *My Art*.)

7. Type a description in the Description edit box (we entered *Mountain Peaks*), and then click the Add button. Here is the resulting dialog box:

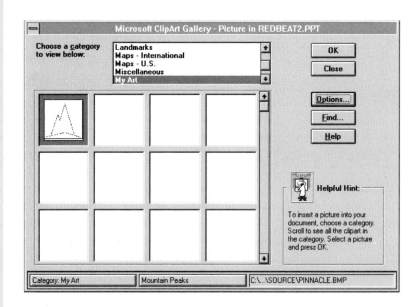

If your graphic is large, it may take a few minutes for PowerPoint to add it to the ClipArt Gallery.

8. Click Close to close the Gallery.

Now, whenever we want to insert the PINNACLE.BMP graphic, we can simply click the Insert Clip Art button on the Standard toolbar, and select the graphic from the Microsoft ClipArt Gallery.

Using PowerPoint's Drawing Tools

In addition to the Drawing toolbar that appears by default in Slide view (and Notes Pages view, see page 153), PowerPoint provides the Drawing+ toolbar. You can use the buttons on both toolbars to draw graphic objects on your PowerPoint slides. A detailed discussion of all the drawing tools is beyond the scope of this book, so we'll show you a simple example and then leave you to explore on your own.

Before you get started drawing objects, take a minute or two to set up your screen, like this:

1. Be sure Slide 1 of REDBEAT2.PPT is displayed in Slide view, click any displayed toolbar with the right mouse button, and choose Drawing+ from the shortcut menu. (You can also choose the Toolbars command from the View menu, and select the Drawing+ option in the Toolbars dialog box.)

2. Next, if the rulers are not already displayed, choose Ruler from the View menu, and then choose Guides from the View menu. (The guides are horizontal and vertical lines that cross the slide and help you position your drawings.) Your screen now looks like this:

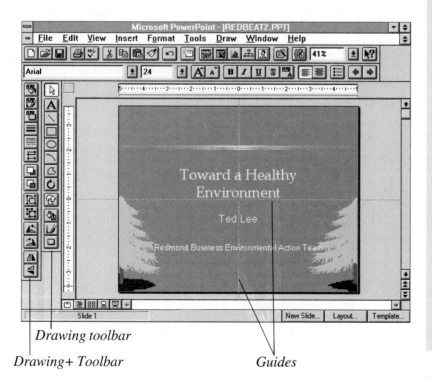

Drawing toolbar

Drawing+ Toolbar   *Guides*

AutoShapes

You can use PowerPoint's Auto-Shapes toolbar to add more complex shapes to your slides. For example, you can add a star by clicking the Star Tool button or add an octagon by clicking the Octagon Tool button. To activate the AutoShapes toolbar, point to any displayed toolbar, click the right mouse button, and choose AutoShapes from the shortcut menu (or choose Toolbars from the View menu, and select the AutoShapes option). The Auto-Shapes toolbar appears as a floating toolbar, which you can move by dragging its title bar. To add an AutoShape, simply click the shape you want, position the mouse pointer on the slide, hold down the left mouse button, and drag the shape into place. You can then resize the shape by dragging its handles, or reposition the shape by pointing to its border and dragging it to a new location. If the AutoShape comes equipped with an *adjustment handle*—a diamond-shaped handle—you can drag that handle to adjust the shape's most prominent characteristic. (For example, you can change the angle of an isosceles triangle by dragging its adjustment handle.) To quickly replace an AutoShape, select the shape, choose Change AutoShape from the Draw menu, and select a different shape from the drop-down palette of AutoShapes.

Using the guides

You can drag the guides to position them where you need them. As you drag, the guide's distance from the corresponding ruler's zero mark is displayed so that you can use the guide to precisely position objects on the slide. For example, to position a rectangle exactly 1 inch above and 2 inches below a slide's center, you must first drag the horizontal guide to the 1-inch mark on the vertical ruler, and draw the rectangle from the guide to approximately the 2-inch mark on the vertical ruler (the 2-inch mark below the zero mark). Then drag the horizontal guide to exactly the 2-inch mark, and align the bottom edge of the rectangle with the guide. To check how far you are dragging the guide across the slide, rather than how far the guide is from the ruler's zero mark, hold down the Ctrl key as you drag the guide.

3. Use ToolTips to get an idea of the functions of the buttons on the Drawing toolbars.

You can draw a number of basic shapes, including lines, rectangles, and squares, using the tools on the Drawing toolbars. To get a feel for drawing shapes and working with the Drawing toolbars, follow the steps below:

1. With Slide 1 displayed in Slide view, click the Ellipse Tool button on the Drawing toolbar.

2. Position the mouse pointer, which is in the shape of a cross, above and to the left of *Ted Lee*.

3. Hold down the left mouse button, and drag to the right and down, until the ellipse obscures *Ted Lee*.

4. With the ellipse selected (surrounded by handles), click the Fill Color button on the Drawing+ toolbar, and select the Shaded option to display this dialog box:

Additional shapes

By holding down the Ctrl and Shift keys while you use certain toolbar buttons, you can create additional shapes. For example, if you hold down Ctrl and Shift while using the Ellipse Tool button, you can create a circle.

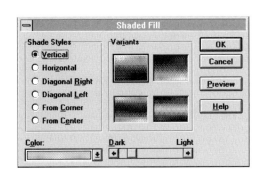

Note that you can change the color of the fill from this dialog box, as well as adjust the intensity of the shading.

5. In the Shade Styles section of the Shaded Fill dialog box, select the From Center option. In the Variants section, check that the top left option is selected, and then click OK.

6. Now click the Line On/Off button on the Drawing toolbar to remove the border surrounding the ellipse.

7. The ellipse is stacked on top of the words *Ted Lee* on the slide. To move the ellipse behind *Ted Lee*, click the Send Backward button on the Drawing+ toolbar a couple of times until *Ted Lee* is visible. (You can click the Bring Forward button to bring a selected object to the top of the stack. For example, if you have five objects in a stack and you want to move the third object to the top of the stack, select the top object, press Tab until the third object is selected, and then click the Bring Forward button twice.)

8. If necessary, use the mouse (and the guides) to reposition the ellipse so that it's centered over *Ted Lee*, and then click anywhere outside the ellipse to deselect it.

9. Turn off the rulers and the guides to see these results:

With all the clip art supplied by PowerPoint, as well as graphics from other applications and PowerPoint's drawing tools, you shouldn't have any trouble adding a dash of excitement to your presentations. Just remember to keep it simple; otherwise, your audience might start paying more attention to your artwork than to the content of your presentation.

Rotating, flipping, and aligning objects

You can use the Free Rotate Tool button on the Drawing toolbar or the Free Rotate command on the Rotate/Flip submenu of the Draw menu to rotate an object about its center. Simply select the object, click the toolbar button or choose the command, point to one of the object's corner handles, and drag to the left or right. If you want to rotate an object exactly 90 degrees to the left or right, select the object, and then either click the Rotate Left or Rotate Right button on the Drawing+ toolbar or choose the appropriate command from the Rotate/Flip submenu. To flip objects horizontally or vertically, select an object, and click the Flip Horizontal or Flip Vertical button on the Drawing+ toolbar or choose the equivalent command from the Rotate/Flip submenu of the Draw menu. Finally you can align several objects on a slide in various ways by selecting the objects, choosing Align from the Draw menu, and then choosing one of the commands from the Align submenu.

6

Teamwork:
Using PowerPoint with Other Applications

We imported a Microsoft Word 6 outline
as the basis for this presentation.
We then selected a template, formatted the title slide,
and wrapped text around the globe using WordArt.
The graphs on Slides 4 and 6 were imported from Microsoft Excel.

Redmond Business Environmental Action Team

Doing what we can
Today
To care for the world of
Tomorrow

What is Redmond BEAT?

- ✦ A local chapter of USA BEAT
- ✦ A network of companies who are actively working to ensure that their business operations are based on sound environmental practices

How does it work?

- ✦ Scrutinize operations
- ✦ Implement procedures that will minimize any adverse effects on the environment
- ✦ Field-test new "environmentally kind" products and services to evaluate their potential impact on both company costs and the environment

When was it started?

- ✦ Redmond BEAT -1989
- ✦ USA BEAT (210 local chapters) - 1987

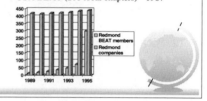

Why was it started?

- ✦ William Henry, President of Creative GlassWorks, wanted less packaging material in his dumpsters
- ✦ Jordan Manufacturing explored alternative packaging methods with good results
- ✦ Henry learned about USA BEAT and campaigned for a Redmond chapter

Who can join?

- ✦ Any company licensed to do business in the city of Redmond

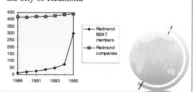

Why should my company join?

- ✦ Be a part of the effort to preserve this area's natural beauty
- ✦ Be perceived as a "green" company by consumers who are increasingly environmentally aware

How can I find out more?

- ✦ Meetings at 8:00 AM on the last Tuesday of every month in the Community Center
- ✦ Contact Ted Lee at 555-6789

In Chapter 5, you imported clip art that had been created in a graphics program. The images were saved in the graphics program in a format that can be used by other programs, including PowerPoint. This kind of transferability of files is nothing new. Almost all full-featured business software products, including word processors, spreadsheets, and databases as well as presentation programs, provide this capability. However, because you can buy PowerPoint not only as a stand-alone product but also as part of the Microsoft Office suite of applications, it has been designed to work with the other suite members—Word, Excel, and Mail—and offers a level of integration that goes way beyond a simple transferability of files.

Microsoft Office Standard or Professional

For this chapter only, we assume that you have Microsoft Office Standard or Professional installed on your computer. (You'll notice slight differences in the screen shots for this chapter because the other six chapters show the screens from stand-alone PowerPoint. If you have the stand-alone version of PowerPoint, you can still read through this chapter to get an idea of the efficiency that can be achieved by using a suite of compatible programs such as Microsoft Office.) We also assume that you are proficient in the use of Word and Excel. (If you're not, *A Quick Course in Word 6 for Windows* and *A Quick Course in Excel 5 for Windows* will bring you quickly up to speed.)

PowerPoint, Word, and Excel

If you have purchased these three applications separately (not as Microsoft Office), you can work through the examples in this chapter, but you will not be able to display the Office Manager toolbar. Instead, you can activate the Microsoft toolbar by pointing to any displayed toolbar, clicking the right mouse button, and then choosing Microsoft from the shortcut menu. (You can also choose Toolbars from the View menu, and then select the Microsoft option in the Toolbars dialog box.)

While working through the examples in this chapter, you will need to start the necessary applications and switch from one application to another. If you have installed Microsoft Office, the most efficient way to work with other Microsoft applications is to use the buttons on the Office Manager toolbar. If this toolbar is not currently displayed in the application title bar at the top of your screen, take a moment to display it now:

1. With PowerPoint active, hold down the Alt key and press Tab until *Program Manager* appears in the box in the center of the screen, and then release the Alt key.

2. Double-click the Microsoft Office icon in the Microsoft Office group window to display the Office Manager toolbar.

3. Use Alt+Tab to switch back to PowerPoint with this toolbar still displayed in the title bar, like this:

Office Manager toolbar

If you haven't seen this toolbar before, you might want to use ToolTips to identify the buttons.

Basing a Presentation on a Word Outline

One of the sample documents used in *A Quick Course in Word 6 for Windows* is background information about Redmond BEAT, which was sent out to companies interested in joining the organization. Suppose you now want to create a general-purpose presentation covering much of the same background information. Instead of having to create the presentation from scratch, you can edit the backgrounder in Word and then import its outline into a PowerPoint presentation. Sound like magic? Let's see how it's done.

You start Word 6 and load the backgrounder document. You then choose Outline from the View menu to switch to Outline view, and edit the outline to include only the headings you want. Follow these steps to create this outline so that you can follow along with the example:

1. Start Word on your computer by clicking the Microsoft Word button on the Office Manager toolbar, and if necessary, maximize the Word window.

2. Switch to Outline view, and enter the first and second level headings shown on the next page.

Creating a Word outline

Creating Word outlines

The first step toward creating an outline in Word is to switch to Outline view by clicking the Outline View button at the bottom of the Document window or by choosing Outline from Word's View menu. Word's Outlining toolbar then appears at the top of the Document window. If you already have a document open, Word also displays various symbols next to the text of the document. A plus sign indicates that subordinate text follows a paragraph; a minus sign indicates no subordinate text; and a small hollow square indicates body text (as opposed to a heading). If you are creating an outline from scratch, Word simply displays a paragraph mark with a minus sign next to it. You can then type the text of the outline, using the buttons on the Outlining toolbar to organize the text by assigning levels to the paragraphs. For example, you can assign a heading level to a body text paragraph by clicking anywhere in the paragraph and then clicking the Promote button. (Depending on the number of heading levels you in your outline, repeatedly clicking the Promote button elevates the heading level of the paragraph.) You can also convert a heading paragraph to body text by clicking anywhere in the paragraph and then clicking the Demote To Body Text button. To find out what the other Outlining toolbar buttons do, use ToolTips.

Redmond Business Environmental Action Team

What is Redmond BEAT?

A local chapter of USA BEAT

A network of companies who are actively working to ensure that their business operations are based on sound environmental practices

How does it work?

Scrutinize operations

Implement procedures that will minimize any adverse effects on the environment

Field-test new "environmentally kind" products and services to evaluate their potential impact on both company costs and the environment

When was it started?

Redmond BEAT -1989

USA BEAT (210 local chapters) - 1987

Why was it started?

William Henry, President of Creative GlassWorks, wanted less packaging material in his dumpsters

Jordan Manufacturing explored alternative packaging methods with good results

Henry learned about USA BEAT and campaigned for a Redmond chapter

Who can join?

Any company licensed to do business in the the city of Redmond

Why should my company join?

Be a part of the effort to preserve this area's natural beauty

Be perceived as a "green" company by consumers who are increasingly environmentally aware

How can I find out more?

Meetings at 8:00 AM on the last Tuesday of every month in the Community Center

Contact Ted Lee at 555-6789

3. Save the document as RECRUIT.DOC, and double-click the Control menu icon at the left end of the application title bar

to close both the document and Word. (Click No if Word asks whether you want to save Document1.)

Now let's import the RECRUIT.DOC outline as a PowerPoint presentation:

1. Back in PowerPoint, make sure you have a new blank presentation open. Click the New button on the Standard toolbar, select the Blank Presentation option in the New Presentation dialog box, and click OK. Then, in the New Slide dialog box, click OK to create the first slide with the default Title Slide layout.)

2. Choose the Slides From Outline command from the Insert menu to display this dialog box:

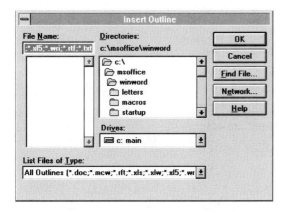

3. Locate the RECRUIT.DOC file, select it, and click OK to use its outline as a basis for the presentation. PowerPoint displays a message box to let you know that it is converting the file. When the conversion process is finished, nothing seems to have changed, but in fact PowerPoint has appended slides based on RECRUIT.DOC to the current presentation.

4. Choose the Delete Slide command from the Edit menu to delete the slide now on your screen and display the first slide of the presentation.

5. Save the presentation as RECRUIT.PPT, assigning *Today/Tomorrow* as the Summary Info title and *General Presentation* as the subject.

Dragging Word text into PowerPoint

If you've spent a lot of time creating a document, such as an outline, in Word and you want to use the same document in a PowerPoint presentation, you don't have to retype the document text in PowerPoint. Instead, you can simply drag the text from Word to PowerPoint. First open both Word and PowerPoint, and then arrange their windows side by side. Be sure the text you want to drag is displayed in the Word window and that Slide view is active in the PowerPoint window. Then select the Word text, and drag the selection to the current PowerPoint slide. (To copy the text rather than move it, hold down the Ctrl key as you drag.) The Word text appears as a picture in PowerPoint, so you can resize and reposition it using the mouse. You cannot edit the text directly in PowerPoint. Instead, you must double-click the text picture to return to Word. The text appears in a frame, complete with rulers, and Word's menus and toolbars are displayed at the top of the screen. You can then edit the text in the usual way. When you're finished, click anywhere outside the frame to return to PowerPoint. If you'd rather edit the text in a separate Word window, click the text picture with the right mouse button, and choose Open Document Object from the shortcut menu. To return to PowerPoint, choose Update from Word's File menu, and then choose Close And Return To *Presentation* from Word's File menu.

6. Before you go any further, dress up the presentation by applying a template. Click the Template button at the bottom of the Presentation window, select INTLC.PPT from the CLROVRHD directory, and click the Apply button. When you return to the Presentation window, the first slide looks like this:

7. Use the Next Slide and Previous Slide buttons at the bottom of the vertical scroll bar to step through the presentation a slide at a time, noticing that PowerPoint has automatically assigned first level headings from the Word outline as slide titles and second level headings as bulleted items.

Using WordArt for Fancy Type Effects

This presentation is quite "presentable" as it is, except that the title slide needs to grab more attention. As you'll see in this section, you can do a lot by changing the font and the font size, adjusting the relative positions of objects on the slide, and balancing the objects against each other by varying the alignment. But for those occasions when you need something more, you can turn to WordArt, a separate program that comes with Word for Windows. With WordArt, you can mold text into various shapes to fit the mood of a presentation or to flow around other elements on a slide. We'll start by making a few simple changes:

1. Turn on the rulers by choosing Ruler from the View menu.

2. With Slide 1 displayed on your screen, click the object area, and then click its frame to select it. Drag the right center handle to the left until the marker on the horizontal ruler is at the 1 1/2-inch mark, and drag the top center handle down until the marker on the vertical ruler is at the 0 mark.

Sizing and positioning the object area

3. Click an insertion point in the object area, type *Doing what we can*, press Shift+Enter to start a new line without starting a new bullet, type *Today*, press Shift+Enter, type *To care for the world of*, press Shift+Enter, and type *Tomorrow*.

4. Select the text, and change its size to 36 points.

5. Choose Bullet from the Format menu to display the Bullet dialog box, click the Use A Bullet option in the top left corner to turn it off, and click OK. Then point to the bottom (left indent) triangle on the horizontal ruler, and drag it to the left so that it is aligned with the top (first-line indent) triangle.

Deleting bullets

6. Next click the title, and then click the title area's frame to select it. Point to the top of the frame (not the handle), and move it down until the marker in the vertical ruler is at the 2 1/2-inch mark.

7. Select the *R* in *Redmond*, and change its size to 60 points. Then repeat this step for the first letters of the other four words in the title. Here are the results:

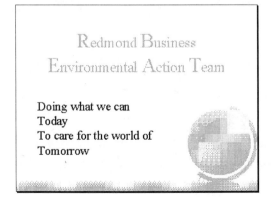

Formatting WordArt objects

The menus and Formatting toolbar that appear at the top of your screen when you're working in WordArt offer a wide variety of formatting options. For example, you can add shading, a shadow, and a border to your WordArt text by clicking the appropriate buttons on the Formatting toolbar (the three buttons at the right end of the toolbar) or by choosing one of the corresponding commands from the Format menu. If you want to increase or decrease the amount of space between characters, you can click the Character Spacing button on the toolbar (the button with the letters *AV* underscored by a double-headed arrow) or choose Spacing Between Characters from the Format menu, and then select the appropriate options in the Spacing Between Characters dialog box. To change the font or font size of your WordArt text, use the Font and Font Size drop-down lists on the Formatting toolbar. To add bold, italic, make the height of all the characters even, flip the text, or stretch the text, click one of the five buttons to the right of the Font Size box. The button that sits all alone on the Formatting toolbar lets you change the alignment of the text, and the button with the circular arrow displays the Special Effects dialog box, which you can use to change the rotation and shape of the text.

Embedding a WordArt Object

Now for something a little fancier. Let's wrap the words *Today* and *Tomorrow* around the globe in the bottom right corner to echo the slide's subtitle. Here are the steps:

1. Choose Object from the Insert menu to display the Insert Object dialog box:

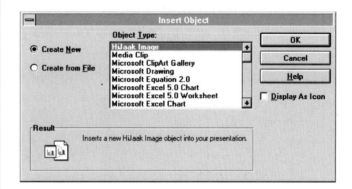

In this dialog box, you select the type of object you want to insert according to the program used to create it.

2. Scroll the Object Type list, and double-click the Microsoft WordArt 2.0 option. PowerPoint opens this window in which you can type the text you want to work with:

3. Type *Today - Tomorrow*, and click Update Display. Your text replaces the placeholder in the frame above.

Here's how to wrap the text around the globe:

1. Click the arrow to the right of Plain Text at the left end of WordArt's Formatting toolbar to display this palette of the available text shapes:

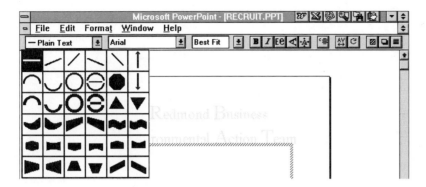

2. Select the first option in the second row. The text in the frame curves into the selected shape.

Shaping WordArt text

3. Now choose Rotation And Effects from WordArt's Format menu to display this dialog box:

Rotating WordArt text

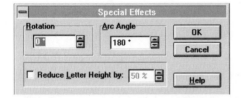

4. Change the setting in the Rotation edit box to –63, and then click OK. PowerPoint rotates your text 63 degrees to the left.

5. Now click anywhere outside the WordArt window and the frame to return to PowerPoint with your text embedded in the title slide of the current presentation.

6. Next you need to size and position the text. First, make sure the setting in the Zoom Control box is 41% (if it's not, change it so that your settings mirror ours). Then point anywhere inside the invisible frame delineated by the black handles, and drag the WordArt object to the right and down as far as it will go. Point to the top left handle, and drag in and down, sizing the frame proportionally until the marker on the horizontal ruler is at about the –1/2-inch mark (the 1/2-inch mark to the left of the 0 mark) and the one on the vertical ruler is at about the 0 mark. Finally, point to the bottom left handle, and drag in and up until the marker on the horizontal ruler is at about the 3/8-inch mark and the marker on the vertical ruler is at about the 3 1/8-inch mark. The text should now curve around the globe, as shown on the next page.

Editing WordArt objects

After a WordArt object has been embedded on a PowerPoint slide, you can return to the WordArt window for editing purposes by double-clicking the object. When you have finished editing, click anywhere outside the WordArt window and frame to return to PowerPoint.

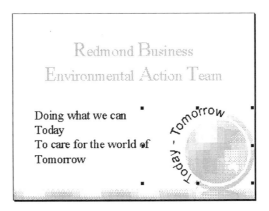

7. Click outside the frame to admire the results, and then save RECRUIT.PPT.

Importing an Excel Graph and Source Data

In Chapter 3, we showed you how to add a graph to a slide using Microsoft Graph. But what if the graph already exists as part of a Microsoft Excel workbook? Or perhaps the graph itself doesn't exist in Excel but the source data does. Instead of having to recreate the graph or its data, you can import it.

Embedding a Graph

As a demonstration, assume that you have created a simple graph in Microsoft Excel that plots the number of companies who are members of Redmond BEAT against the number licensed to do business in the city of Redmond. Follow these steps to create this graph so that you can follow along with the example:

1. Click the Microsoft Excel button on the Office Manager toolbar to start Excel, and then enter the following data:

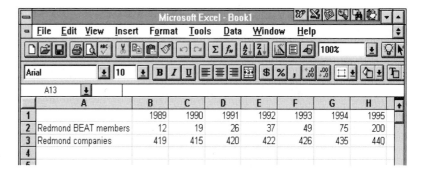

2. Select the cell range A1:H3, click the ChartWizard button on Excel's Standard toolbar, and drag a rectangle from cell B5 through cell F17. Then work your way through the Chart-Wizard dialog boxes, selecting the Line graph type in the second dialog box and the first format in the third dialog box, and accepting all the other defaults. When you click Finish, Excel plots the graph in the rectangle.

Creating an Excel graph

3. Click the graph with the right mouse button, choose Format Object from the shortcut menu, click the None option in the Border section of the Patterns tab, and click OK to turn off the border surrounding the graph.

Removing the graph's border

4. Save the workbook with the name REDBEAT.XLS, assigning *Membership* as the title and *Annual Growth* as the subject in the Summary Info dialog box. Then double-click the Control menu icon at the left end of the application title bar to close both the document and Excel.

Let's embed the graph in the RECRUIT.PPT presentation:

1. Move to Slide 6 of RECRUIT.PPT, choose Object from the Insert menu, select Microsoft Excel 5.0 Chart, and then click the Create From File option. PowerPoint changes the options in the Insert Object dialog box like this, so that you can identify the workbook file containing the graph:

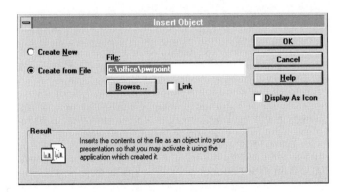

2. Click an insertion point at the end of the File edit box, type *redbeat.xls*, and press Enter. PowerPoint closes the dialog box, and after a few seconds, embeds the requested worksheet in the slide, as shown on the next page.

Formatting embedded Excel graphs

To format an Excel graph that has been embedded on a PowerPoint slide, you must first return to Excel by double-clicking the graph in PowerPoint. Then, back in Excel, double-click the graph again to open Microsoft Graph, which provides all the tools you need to format the graph. For more information about Micro-soft Graph's formatting capabilities, see Chapter 3.

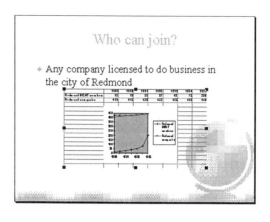

Embedding an Excel worksheet

You can embed an Excel worksheet on a PowerPoint slide by clicking the Insert Microsoft Excel Worksheet button on PowerPoint's Standard toolbar, and dragging across the columns and down the rows in the grid that appears to specify the number of columns and rows you want in the worksheet. A worksheet surrounded by a frame then appears on the current slide, and Excel's menus and toolbars are displayed at the top of the screen. You can enter data and format the worksheet just as you would normally in Excel. When the worksheet is complete, be sure all the cells you want included in the embedded worksheet are visible within the worksheet frame, and then click anywhere outside the frame to embed the worksheet as a picture on the current PowerPoint slide.Because the worksheet is a picture, you can resize and reposition it using the mouse. If you want to edit the worksheet, you must return to Excel by double-clicking the worksheet.

3. Save the presentation.

How do you make the extraneous worksheet information go away? You can crop the image by changing the size of the frame without changing the size of the image, the same way you cropped graphics in Chapter 5. Try this:

1. Click the worksheet with the right mouse button, and choose Crop Picture from the shortcut menu. The mouse pointer changes to the cropping icon.

2. Point to the right center handle, and drag inward until the object's frame is just inside the chart area. Repeat this step with the center handles on the other three sides so that the frame no longer displays anything but the graph. Then click outside the slide to change the pointer from the cropping icon back to an arrow.

You can easily adjust the position and size of the graph, using these familiar techniques:

1. Click the graph, and drag the left center handle to the left until the marker on the horizontal ruler is at −4, drag the top center handle until the marker on the vertical ruler is at 7/8, and drag the bottom center handle until the marker on the vertical ruler is at −3 3/8. Make any other adjustments that are necessary to position and size the graph as shown here:

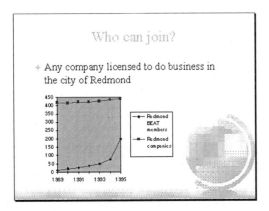

Editing the Graph

The embedded graph is not linked to the Excel worksheet that created it, but the data is available from within PowerPoint, so if you need to edit the graph on the slide, you can. As an example, suppose you want to revise your target of 200 members for 1995 to 300. Follow these steps to see how to make this change to the graph:

1. Double-click the graph. PowerPoint opens a window in which it displays the Excel worksheet containing the graph's underlying data, like this:

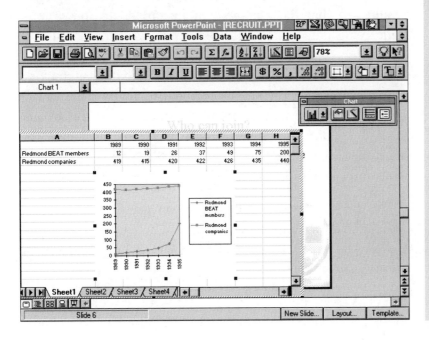

Dragging an Excel worksheet into PowerPoint

Like Word text, you can drag an Excel worksheet directly onto a PowerPoint slide. Just arrange the Excel and PowerPoint windows side by side. (Be sure Slide view is active.) Then select the worksheet range in the Excel window, position the mouse pointer on the border surrounding the range, and drag the range to the slide in the PowerPoint window. (If you want to copy the range, rather than move it, hold down the Ctrl key as you drag.) The worksheet appears as a picture on the slide, which you can resize and move with the mouse. If you want to edit the worksheet, double-click it. The worksheet is then displayed inside a frame on the current slide, and Excel's menus and toolbars appear at the top of the screen. If you want to edit the worksheet in a separate Excel window, click the worksheet with the right mouse button, and choose Open Worksheet Object from the shortcut menu. When you're finished, return to PowerPoint by choosing Update from Excel's File menu and then choosing Exit And Return To *Presentation* from Excel's File menu.

Notice that the toolbars and menu bar have changed to give you access to Excel commands and features, just as if you had started the program manually. You are in fact working with Excel from within PowerPoint.

Automatic updating

2. Change the data in the 1995 column of the Redmond BEAT Members row from 200 to 300, and click outside the window. As you can see here, PowerPoint updates the graph on the slide to reflect the data adjustment:

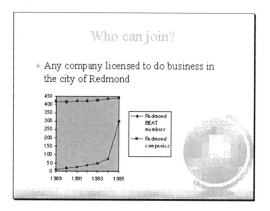

Importing Excel Source Data

If you started Excel and loaded REDBEAT.XLS now, you would see that the change you just made to the graph's underlying data is not reflected in the worksheet you used when embedding the graph. If you want this kind of dynamic link to be maintained between the graph and its source work-sheet, you use a different method of creating the graph. Instead of embedding the graph as an object, you copy and paste the source data into a Microsoft Graph datasheet, cre-ating the link during the pasting process. Follow these steps to see how this process works:

Linking the graph and its data

1. Click the Microsoft Excel button on the Office Manager toolbar, and then choose REDBEAT.XLS from the bottom of Excel's File menu to load the workbook you used for the previous example.

2. Select A1:H3, click the Copy button on Excel's Standard toolbar to store the information on the Windows Clipboard.

3. Click the Microsoft PowerPoint button on the Office Manager toolbar to switch to PowerPoint. Then move to Slide 4 of RECRUIT.PPT, and choose the Microsoft Graph command from the Insert menu.

4. When the datasheet opens, click the blank cell in the top left corner, and choose Paste Link from Graph's Edit menu. Then click OK when PowerPoint warns that the new data will overwrite the existing data. PowerPoint pastes the data copied from REDBEAT.XLS into the datasheet and displays the ChartWizard dialog box.

5. Click OK to accept the default settings, and then click outside the datasheet to view the graph.

6. Resize the graph so that it looks like this:

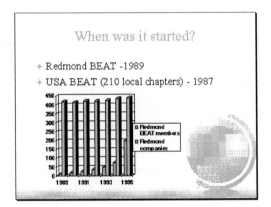

Editing the Source Data

Now again suppose that you want to change the membership target for 1995. Follow these steps to adjust the target:

1. Switch to Excel, and change 200 to 300 in the 1995 column of the Redmond BEAT Members row.

2. Save your edit, and quit Excel.

3. Back in PowerPoint, Slide 4 of RECRUIT.PPT reflects the change you just made to the underlying data source.

We hope that this quick overview will inspire you to explore other methods of exchanging information among the Microsoft Office applications. Your efficiency will increase dramatically as you take advantage of these integrated programs.

Routing a presentation with Mail

If you have Microsoft Mail installed on your computer, you can send your presentation to colleagues for review. First open the presentation in PowerPoint, and choose the Send command from the File menu. Then, in the Send Mail dialog box, identify the person to whom you want to send the presentation, and click the Send button. PowerPoint attaches the presentation to a note and forwards it to the specified recipient. If you want to send the presentation to more than one person, choose the Add Routing Slip command from the File menu instead of the Send command.

7

Center Stage:
Putting on a Show

*We use RECYCLE.PPT to show you how to add transitions
and build effects, hide a slide with supporting information,
and branch to a subordinate slide.
We show you how to use PowerPoint to determine how long
each slide should be displayed, and we generate speaker's notes.*

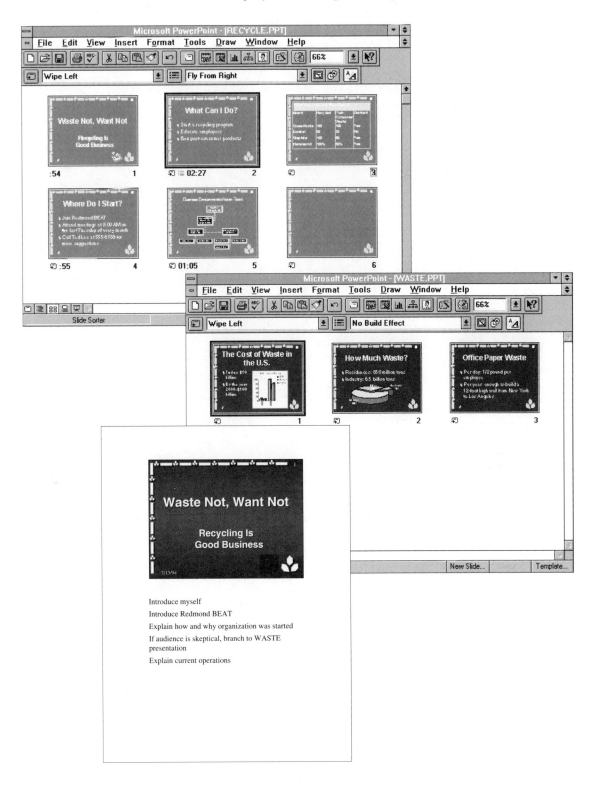

In previous chapters, we've created presentations that were destined to be produced as overheads and 35mm slides. These two familiar formats are used most frequently by people who give presentations only occasionally. They require very little equipment, and that equipment is inexpensive and commonly available. However, a third format, the electronic slide show, is gaining in popularity, partly because being able to deliver an electronic slide show conveys an impression of being "up" on the latest technology, and partly because electronic slide shows allow you to interact with your presentation in ways that are not possible with static overheads and 35mm slides. Because the slide show is delivered from the computer, it can incorporate special effects, such as the wipes and fades associated with video and television productions, and can skip slides or branch off in new directions as appropriate. An electronic slide show can even incorporate audio, video, and animation segments developed with other programs and can be set to run automatically, either at a predefined pace that keeps it in synch with a presenter or independently, as a stand-alone presentation.

Electronic slide shows take more thought to prepare than overheads and 35mm slides—at least, the first slide show does—because you need to carefully consider the hardware aspects of the presentation. With overheads and 35mm slides, you usually show up for your presentation with a folder of transparencies or a carousel of slides ready to dim the lights and get right to the point. Things aren't quite so simple with an electronic slide show. For one thing, the type of equipment you use varies with the size and nature of your audience, and for another, the potential for something to be missing or incompatible varies with the complexity of the equipment. For this reason, we start this chapter with a quick look at what you need in the way of hardware to give a successful electronic slide show.

Equipment for Electronic Slide Shows

The first thing to consider when you decide to develop an electronic slide show is how you plan to give your presentation. Will your audience be coming to you or will you be doing the traveling? Will you be making your presentation on your own computer or someone else's? Whenever possible, it is wise to control as many variables as you can by developing the presentation on the computer you will be using to deliver the slide show. Otherwise, you can spend hours fine-tuning a dynamic presentation on a 486 DX2 60 MHz machine with 16 MB of RAM for a conference in a distant city, only to find that the laptop provided by the conference organizers is a 486 SX 25 MHz machine with 4 MB of RAM. If you can't take your computer with you, try to find out what kind of computer will be available so that you can make allowances for any major differences.

The computer

The next question to consider is the size of your audience. Will you be making your presentation to a cozy group of less than five people around a conference table, a seminar of 30 people, or an auditorium of 100 or more? Although the intimate group might not mind crowding around a regular 14-inch or 15-inch computer screen, for the larger groups you are going to need a larger image. If you don't want to dim the lights and curtail audience interaction, you might try a monitor of 20 inches or more for a small seminar, but for most occasions when you are addressing a room full of people, you will need either an LCD panel or an LCD projector to get your point across clearly.

The image

An LCD panel is a flat screen that plugs into your computer and displays a duplicate of the image you see on your computer's monitor. You lay the panel on an overhead projector to project that image onto a standard slide screen. The resolution of the image is determined by the type of panel and by the brightness of the overhead projector. An active matrix panel with an overhead projector of 3000 to 4000 lumens is quite adequate for an audience of 50 or more people. Even with the highest resolution, though, the colors projected with the panel may not appear the same as those on your computer's screen, so it's best not to use LCD panels in situations where precise colors are important (fashion design and interior decorating are examples that come to mind). An LCD projector operates on a similar principle, except that a light source and lens are built into the hardware. A good quality projector can project clear images for an audience of up to 300 people, but high quality projectors with active matrix

LCD panels

LCD projectors

displays and other image-enhancing features are expensive. Lower quality projectors cost less but can produce poor images that do nothing but annoy audiences.

Renting equipment

For occasional use, you might be better off renting the equipment you need, but be careful that all cables and other accessories are included with the primary hardware. If you are renting locally and transporting the equipment to the presentation site, put everything together and test for compatibility before you leave, allowing time to return to the rental company for missing or replacement parts if necessary. If someone else is in charge of setting up your equipment, check with them ahead of time to make sure there are no misunderstandings about your equipment needs.

We'll talk more about the logistics of preparing for an electronic slide show later in this chapter, but for now, with this discussion of basic equipment out of the way, we'll take a look at some of the elements you can add to an electronic slide show to take advantage of this presentation medium.

Viewing a Slide Show

There are two ways to deliver an electronic slide show: with PowerPoint and with PowerPoint Viewer. We cover the ins and outs of PowerPoint Viewer on page 158. Here, we'll assume that you want to give an electronic slide show from PowerPoint itself. You do this by switching to Slide Show view, which expands your slides to fill the entire screen, obscuring PowerPoint window elements such as the title bar and toolbars. Let's experiment with Slide Slow view using the RECYCLE.PPT presentation you developed in earlier chapters:

1. If necessary, start PowerPoint, and then locate and open RECYCLE.PPT.

Changing the type of output

2. You'll recall that RECYCLE.PPT was designed to be produced as 35mm slides, so before you go any further, you need to change the type of output. Choose Slide Setup from the File menu to display this dialog box:

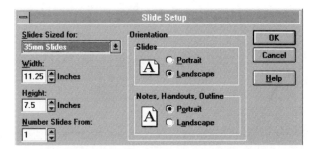

3. Click the arrow to the right of the Slides Sized For edit box, select On-Screen Show from the drop-down list (the Width setting changes from 11.25 to 10), and click OK.

4. Now click the Slide Show button at the bottom of the Presentation window to display the title slide of the presentation in Slide Show view, like this:

5. To move to the next slide, click the left mouse button.

6. Continue clicking the left mouse button to step through the slides one at a time.

If you click the left mouse button when the last slide is displayed, PowerPoint switches back to the view you were in before you clicked the Slide Show button and returns you to the first slide. You can avoid this rather abrupt return to reality by adding a blank slide at the end of the presentation to alert

Adjusting for the presentation output

When you change the type of output for a presentation in the Slide Setup dialog box, some of the elements that you defined in one output type may have shifted on their slides when you display them in the new output type. For example, if the table on Slide 6 is no longer correctly sized for the slide after you switched output types from 35mm Slides to On-Screen Show, simply return to Slide view, adjust the table's size, and click the Slide Show button to see the effects of the adjustment.

you to the fact that you have reached the last slide. Let's add a final slide to the presentation now:

1. In Slide view, scroll to the end of the presentation, and click the New Slide button at the bottom of the Presentation window to add a ninth slide.

2. In the New Slide dialog box, scroll the AutoLayout images so that you can select the last one in the last row (Blank), and click OK.

3. Now go back to the first slide, switch to Slide Show view, and step through the slides again, stopping when you get to the blank slide. A much more graceful ending!

4. Return to Slide view by pressing the Esc key.

Running the Presentation Automatically

Sometimes you might want to move around as you deliver a presentation, or you might want to be able to set the presentation in motion and then forget about it, as with point-of-purchase presentations. Instead of being tied to your mouse, you can set up the slide show to automatically move from one slide to another. Follow these steps to see how this works:

1. Switch to Slide Sorter view, and choose Select All from the Edit menu to select all the slides in the presentation.

2. Click the Transition button on the Slide Sorter toolbar to display this dialog box:

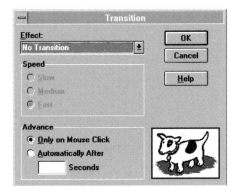

3. We'll work with the Effect and Speed sections of this dialog box in a moment. For now, simply click the Automatically

After option in the Advance section, enter *10* in the Seconds edit box, and click OK. PowerPoint indicates the timings you have set below each slide, like this:

Setting the slide timings

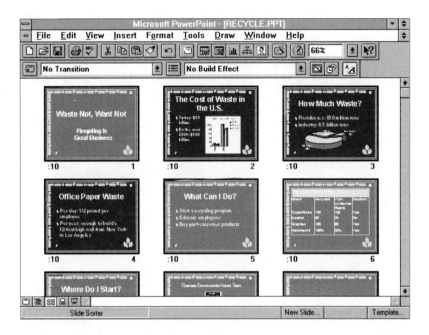

4. Now choose Slide Show from the View menu to display this dialog box:

5. In the Advance section, click the Use Slide Timings option to activate the timings you set in the Transition dialog box, and then click Show. PowerPoint switches to Slide Show view and displays Slide 1. After 10 seconds, it advances to Slide 2, then Slide 3, and so on.

6. Interrupt the show at any time by pressing Esc to return to Slide Sorter view.

Displaying selected slides

If you only want to show specific slides from a presentation during a slide show, choose the Slide Show command from the View menu to display the Slide Show dialog box. Then, in the Slides section of the dialog box, enter the numbers of the slides you want to show in the From and To edit boxes, and click Show. The first of the selected slides instantly appears in Slide Show view. As always, you can use the mouse buttons and the Page-Down and PageUp keys to move through the other slides in the presentation, and then press Esc when you're finished.

Adding Transitions

So far, moving manually from slide to slide in the electronic slide show is no different from moving manually among 35mm slides. However, setting up your presentation as an electronic slide show opens up the potential for using special effects that are not possible with individual 35mm slides. In this section, we'll add a simple transition to move the audience smoothly from slide to slide without the jerkiness associated with the replacement of one slide by another. Here's how to add transitions to all the slides except the title slide:

1. In Slide Sorter view, choose Select All from the Edit menu to select all the slides. Then hold down the Shift key, and click the title slide to deselect it. Now any commands you choose will affect all slides except the title slide.

2. Click the arrow to the right of the Transition Effects box on the Slide Sorter toolbar, select Blinds Vertical from the drop-down list, and watch Slide 2 carefully as PowerPoint demonstrates the effect of the transition you have selected. Notice that PowerPoint displays a transition icon below the slides with transitions.

Testing the transitions

3. Click the title slide to select it. Then switch to Slide Show view, and watch as PowerPoint runs the slide show with the specified transitions.

4. When PowerPoint reaches the blank slide, press Esc to switch back to Slide Sorter view, and experiment with other transition effects. For example, try applying a different effect to each slide—go a little crazy!

Changing the transition speed

5. Next, select Slides 2 and 3, click the Transition button on the Slide Sorter toolbar to display the Transition dialog box, and in the Speed section, click the Slow option, and then click OK. Select Slide 1, and rerun the slide show with the transitions at this new speed.

6. Now apply the Wipe Left transition to all the slides except the title slide, reset the speed to Fast, select Slide 1, and run through the slide show to test these transition settings.

As you've probably realized, it's easy to overdo transitions. Your audience will find these special effects less distracting if you stick to one kind of transition for all your slides and if you stick with the fast speed to keep them focused on the content of your presentation rather than its mechanics.

Adding Build Effects

Another way in which you can take advantage of your computer to raise your presentation above the level of a simple 35mm slide show is to add builds to bulleted list slides. Builds are just what you might think: They build the slide a bulleted item at a time. By using builds, you can keep your audience focused on the point you are making right now, instead of allowing them to read ahead, perhaps diluting the impact of your message. Let's add a build effect to one of the slides in the RECYCLE.PPT presentation to see how they work:

1. In Slide Sorter view, select Slide 5, click the arrow to the right of the Build Effects box, and select Fly From Left from the drop-down list. PowerPoint puts a build icon below Slide 5 to indicate that you have assigned a build effect to this slide.

2. Switch to Slide Show view to test the effect. The slide starts out with just its title, and then PowerPoint moves each bulleted item onto the slide in turn.

Testing the build

3. When the slide show moves to the next slide, return to Slide Sorter view by pressing Esc.

Moving the bulleted items in from the left is somewhat jarring because your eyes are accustomed to reading from left to right, not right to left. You can change the build effect on the toolbar, or you can make this and other changes in the Build dialog box. Follow these steps to display this dialog box:

1. Select Slide 5, and click the Build button on the Slide Sorter toolbar to display the Build dialog box:

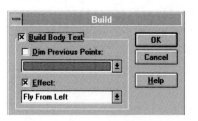

2. Change the Effect option to Fly From Right to make the text move in from the right instead of the left.

Dimming previous bulleted
items

3. Click the Dim Previous Points option, click the arrow to the right of the color box below the option, select the light green color at the right end of the top row, and click OK.

4. Test your changes by switching to Slide Show view. Notice that PowerPoint now changes the color of existing bulleted items as it brings in a new item so that your audience's attention is always focused on the current point.

5. The 10-second display time for this slide now seems a little rushed, so with Slide 5 selected in Slide Sorter view, click the Transition button, change the Automatically After setting in the Advance section to 20, and click OK. Back in Slide Sorter view, PowerPoint has changed the display setting for this slide from 10 to 20.

6. Select Slide 4, and switch to Slide Show view to test the transition to Slide 5, the build effect, and the transition to Slide 6.

Preparing Speaker-Controlled Presentations

The title of this section might surprise you. After all, aren't all presentations delivered by speakers? Not anymore. Presentation programs like PowerPoint now incorporate stand-alone capabilities that you can use to produce self-running presentations. You can mail these presentations to clients or use them as point-of-purchase displays or at trade shows. However, the majority of presentations are still delivered by a live human being, so in this section, we'll cover some of the special effects you can incorporate into a speaker-controlled electronic slide show. We'll also discuss how to produce speaker's notes to guide you, as well as how to rehearse for a presentation.

Adding Interaction

One measure of a good presentation is how well it delivers its message—whether it gets its point across. The design of the presentation itself obviously has a lot to do with its success, but a number of other factors also play a large role, such as the delivery style of the speaker and his or her ability to help the audience grasp the main thrust of the presentation. Also important is the speaker's ability (and willingness) to meet the audience's needs for clarification and more information. In this section, we discuss the PowerPoint features that enable you to maximize the chances that your audience will walk away from your electronic slide show having understood and accepted your message.

Drawing on the Slides

Although you have taken great pains to reduce the words on your slides to the minimum number needed to say what you want to say, during the course of a slide show, you might need to draw attention to a single element on a slide. Just as you can mark up overhead transparencies with a felt-tip marker, you can mark up electronic slides with an on-screen "pencil," and you don't even have to worry about cleaning up the mess afterward.

Suppose you decide that you want to emphasize the dollar amounts on Slide 2 of the RECYCLE.PPT presentation while verbally drawing attention to the percentage increase. Follow these steps to see how to mark up a slide on-the-fly:

1. First, in Slide Sorter view, choose Select All from the Edit menu, click the Transition button, and change the Advance option in the Transition dialog box to Only On Mouse Click so that you can manually move from slide to slide.

Switching to manual advancement

2. Now select Slide 2, and click the Slide Show button.

3. Move the mouse pointer over the slide, and notice that a button with a pencil icon appears in the bottom right corner.

4. Click the pencil button, move the pencil pointer to the first bulleted item, hold down the left mouse button, and draw a circle or square around $10. Then draw a circle or square around $100 in the second bulleted item. The slide now looks as shown on the next page.

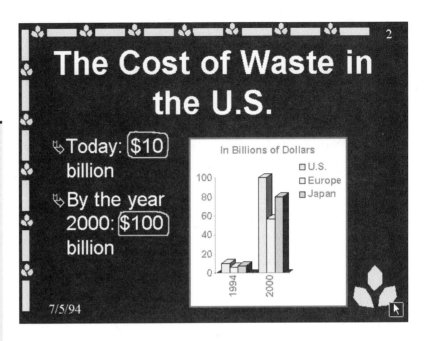

"Drill-down" documents

If you have supporting information in a file created with another Windows application, you can access that information during a PowerPoint slide show by "drilling down" to it. For example, you can drill down to a report created in Word or an inventory list created in Access. The drill-down process takes advantage of OLE (object linking and embedding), so if your application supports OLE, you're in luck. To add a drill-down document to a presentation, you embed the document as an object. First choose Object from the Insert menu, and when the Insert Object dialog box appears, select the Create From File option, and enter the complete pathname for the file in the File edit box. (If you don't know the pathname, click the Browse button, and select the file in the Browse dialog box.) Next, select the Display As Icon option, and click OK. The embedded object is then displayed on the current slide as an icon, and all you have to do to drill down to the document is double-click the icon. The document is displayed in the originating application's window. To return to the presentation, choose Close And Return To *Presentation* (or a similar command) from the drill-down document's File menu.

5. Click the button with the arrow icon in the bottom right corner of the screen to restore the arrow pointer.

Hiding Supporting Information

When someone in your audience requests clarification of a point you are making or questions your assumptions or conclusions, you will usually want to take the time to address their concerns before moving on. If you know your audience well, you can generally predict the kinds of questions they are likely to ask and can touch on those points in your presentation. But if you are unsure of your audience's level of knowledge about your topic or the focus of their interest, you probably won't want to clutter up the presentation with supporting information that your audience may not need. In that case, you might want to put the supporting information on hidden slides. Then if no questions are asked, you can simply skip over them, but if your audience does need more information, you can display the hidden slides to qualify your statements or back them up with hard facts.

In Chapter 4, you added a table slide to the RECYCLE.PPT presentation with information about several types of recycled paper. Suppose you want to hide this slide but keep it in the wings in case someone asks for examples of post-consumer products. Follow these steps to hide Slide 6:

1. Switch to Slide Sorter view, and select Slide 6, the table slide.

2. Click the Hide Slide button on the Slide Sorter toolbar.
PowerPoint indicates that the slide is hidden by putting a slash
through the slide number; it doesn't actually hide the slide.

3. Select Slide 5, switch to Slide Show view, click the left mouse
button three times to build the bullet list, and then move the
mouse pointer over the slide. The pencil button and a hidden
slide button appear in the bottom right corner, like this:

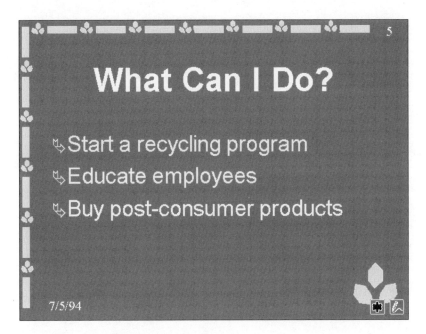

4. Click the left mouse button to move to the next slide. Power-
Point skips over Slide 6 and displays Slide 7.

5. Click the right mouse button to return to Slide 5, move the
mouse pointer to display the hidden slide button, and click
the button. PowerPoint displays the table slide with its information about recycled paper.

6. Click the left mouse button to move to Slide 7, and then click
the right mouse button. PowerPoint takes you to Slide 5; it
does not display the hidden slide when it backs up.

**Returning to a previous
slide**

Branching to a Subordinate Presentation

The ability to hide slides is useful when you want to have
information available in case you need it to make a point.
However, if you want to design a presentation for multiple

audiences, a better alternative might be to build a core presentation and then incorporate other subordinate presentations that meet the needs of different groups. With some careful design work ahead of time, you can break down your presentations into reusable modules so that you can leverage your presentations in multiple directions.

As an example, suppose you want to be able to use Slides 2 through 4 in several presentations. You can copy them from one presentation to another, but an alternate way of accomplishing the same thing without storing multiple copies of these slides in multiple presentations is to store the slides in their own presentation file and then embed the file in each of the presentations where these slides are needed. The first task is to move the slides to their own file. Here are the steps:

Moving slides to a different presentation

1. Switch to Slide Sorter view, click the New button on the Standard toolbar, and in the New Presentation dialog box, click Template, and then click OK. In the Presentation Template dialog box, select TREES.PPT, and click Apply. Accept the default Title Slide AutoLayout by clicking OK in the New Slide dialog box. PowerPoint opens a new presentation in Slide view, completely obscuring RECYCLE.PPT.

2. Click the Slide Sorter View button, and then choose Arrange All from the Window menu. The windows look like this:

Copying slides between presentations

To copy a slide or slides from one presentation to another, first arrange the presentations side by side in Slide Sorter view. Then select the slide or slides you want to copy, hold down the Ctrl key and the left mouse button, and drag the slide to the desired location in the adjacent presentation. You can also use the Copy and Paste buttons on the Standard toolbar or the Copy and Paste commands on the Edit menu to copy slides between presentations. Note that when you copy a slide (or slides) to another presentation, the copied slide takes on the template design of the presentation to which it was copied.

3. Click Slide 2 of RECYCLE.PPT, hold down the Shift key, click Slides 3 and 4 to select all three slides, and release the Shift key.

4. Now point to one of the selected slides, hold down the left mouse button, and drag the slides from the RECYCLE.PPT window into the new presentation's window. Release the button when the insertion point is to the left of the blank title slide. PowerPoint moves all three slides to the new presentation and renumbers the remaining slides in RECYCLE.PPT.

5. Select the blank slide in the new presentation, and press the Delete key to remove it.

6. Now save the new presentation with the name WASTE.PPT, entering *Waste* as the title and *Scary Statistics* as the subject in the Summary Info dialog box.

7. Choose Close from the File menu to close WASTE.PPT, and maximize the RECYCLE.PPT presentation's window.

Closing the presentation

Now you're ready to use WASTE.PPT in other presentations. Follow these steps to embed it in RECYCLE.PPT:

1. Select Slide 1, switch to Slide view, and choose Object from the Insert menu to display the Insert Object dialog box. (The Object command is not available from Slide Sorter view.)

Embedding one presentation in another

2. Scroll the Object Type list, and select MS PowerPoint 4.0 Presentation. Then click the Create From File option, click an insertion point at the end of the entry in the File edit box, and type *waste.ppt*.

3. Now click the Display As Icon option, and click the Change Icon button to display this dialog box:

Selecting an icon

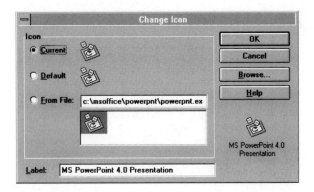

4. The icon itself is fine, but let's get rid of the label. Select the text in the Label edit box, press the Delete key, and click OK twice to return to Slide view, where PowerPoint has inserted a tiny icon.

5. Move, size, and crop the icon until it looks as shown here (see page 111 for information about cropping):

Let's see how PowerPoint handles branching to a subordinate presentation:

1. Switch to Slide Show view, and click the presentation icon. PowerPoint branches to the WASTE.PPT presentation and displays Slide 1.

2. Click the left mouse button twice to step through the remaining WASTE.PPT slides, and click it a third time to return to Slide 1 of RECYCLE.PPT. Then move the pointer away from the presentation icon, and click a fourth time to move on to Slide 2 of RECYCLE.PPT.

Having broken out the "scary statistics" slides into their own file, you can embed them in any presentation and access the slides whenever you need them simply by clicking their icon.

Creating Speaker's Notes

With any presentation, you are probably going to want to jot down a few notes to remind yourself of the points you want to make while displaying each slide. With an electronic slide show, you will also want to include instructions about marking up slides, displaying hidden slides, or branching to subordinate presentations. In PowerPoint, you can generate a notes page for each slide, complete with a thumbnail of the slide itself and any additional information you care to add. Let's create notes pages for the slides in RECYCLE.PPT:

1. If necessary, press the Esc key to return to Slide view, display Slide 1, and then click the Notes Pages View button at the bottom of the Presentation window. PowerPoint displays the notes page for the first slide, like this:

2. Click the arrow to the right of the Zoom Control box on the Standard toolbar, and select 100% from the drop-down list to zoom in on the notes area of the page.

Zooming in on the notes area

3. Click the text object, type *Introduce myself and Redmond BEAT*, press Enter, and type *If skeptical, branch to WASTE presentation.*

4. It's a good idea to make the important words on the page stand out so that you can simply glance at the page rather than having to read it. Select *Introduce*, and click the Bold button, and then repeat this step with *branch* in the second line.

5. Continue adding notes to the notes pages of other slides, experimenting with the formatting options—including bullets and indent levels as well as text styles—available on the Formatting toolbar. (You can also choose the Line Spacing command from the Format menu to vary the space between the notes.)

Audience handouts

If you want to hand out copies of your presentation to an audience, you can use the Handouts options in the Print dialog box. By choosing Print from the File menu and selecting one of the Handouts options from the Print What drop-down list in the Print dialog box, you can print two, three, or six slides on a page. If you want to change the orientation of the slides, choose Slide Setup from the File menu, and select Portrait (vertical) or Landscape (horizontal) in the Notes, Handouts, Outline section of the Slide Setup dialog box.

When you are ready, follow these steps to see how to print the speaker's notes:

Printing notes pages

1. Choose Print from the File menu to display the Print dialog box (see page 25).

2. Click the arrow to the right of the Print What edit box, and select Notes Pages from the drop-down list.

3. Make any necessary changes to the other settings in the dialog box, and then click OK. PowerPoint prints the notes pages in portrait mode (vertically).

Preparing for Delivery

Some people can stand up before a group and deliver an impromptu speech that nevertheless sounds eloquent and well-reasoned. The rest of us must practice, practice, practice. Even if you are an experienced speaker, you will probably want to make sure you are prepared to handle the glitches that can arise with an electronic presentation. A tiny setback can be explained to a sympathetic audience and worked around; an accumulation of setbacks can spell disaster.

The key to avoiding embarrassment is adequate rehearsal. With electronic slide shows, rehearsing takes two forms: one involving the pacing of your presentation, and the other involving logistics. We'll look at both forms in this section.

PowerPoint Rehearsals

The hallmark of a planned presentation is that it starts on time, ends on time, and proceeds at an easy pace in between, accommodating questions and relevant tangents but nevertheless sticking to the topic at hand and telling the audience what they need to know. If you have been allocated 45 minutes to give a presentation and, using a formula of about 2 minutes per slide, you create an electronic slide show of 25 slides, you will probably be uncomfortable if you get to the last slide with 20 minutes to kill. Conversely, if you are only on Slide 20 when your time is up and you have to rush your conclusion, you will probably kick yourself for not having allowed enough time to hammer home your message.

Landscape-mode speaker's notes

By default, speaker's notes appear in portrait mode when printed or when displayed in Notes Pages view. If you want to change the orientation of the notes from portrait (vertical) to landscape (horizontal), choose the Slide Setup command from the File menu, and select the Landscape option in the Notes, Handouts, Outline section of the Slide Setup dialog box.

PowerPoint can't create a powerful presentation for you, but it can help you ensure that the presentation is correctly paced. You have seen how to use the Automatically After setting in the Advance section of the Transition dialog box to have PowerPoint move automatically from one slide to another. Instead of entering an arbitrary number of seconds for this setting as you did earlier, you can have PowerPoint record how long each slide stays on the screen while you rehearse your presentation, and you can then use the recorded time for each slide as its Automatically After setting. This process not only gives you an idea of how long the total presentation is (when you proceed without audience interruption) but means that you can use PowerPoint's advancement through the slides to keep you on track and on time.

To record the slide timings for the RECYCLE.PPT presentation, try this:

1. Switch to Slide Sorter view, and click the Rehearse Timings button on the Slide Sorter toolbar. PowerPoint switches to Slide Show view and displays a digital "stopwatch" ticking away the seconds in the bottom left corner of the slide.

2. Say a few pertinent sentences that are relevant to the title slide of the presentation, and then click the mouse button to move to Slide 2. The digital stopwatch is reset to 0 and begins timing the second slide.

3. Repeat step 2 for the remaining slides.

4. When you reach the blank slide at the end of the presentation, press the Esc key. PowerPoint displays this message box:

5. Make a note of the total time taken for the presentation, and click Yes to both enter the slide timings in the Transition dialog box for each slide and display them in Slide Sorter view, as shown on the next page.

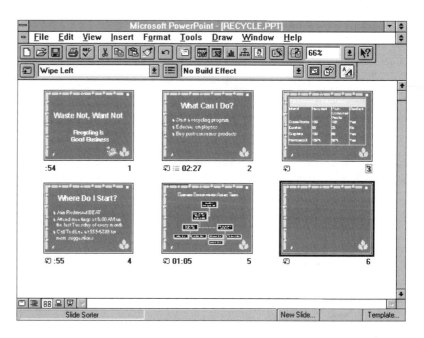

If the total presentation time is too long, you can talk less while each slide is displayed, or you can look for ways to cut the number of slides. If the time is too short, you can talk more while each slide is displayed, or you can add slides. Either way, you can repeat the rehearsal process to enter new timings for each slide until you get the pace of the presentation just right. Then you need to switch from manual to automatic advancement in the Slide Show dialog box, like this:

1. Choose Slide Show from the View menu.

2. In the Slide Show dialog box, check that Use Slide Timings in the Advance section is selected, and then click Show.

3. Rehearse the slide show one more time while PowerPoint runs the slide show.

Pausing the slide show and blanking the screen

If PowerPoint advances to the next slide while you are talking, you can press the S key or the + key on the numeric keypad to pause the slide show and then press the B key to turn the screen black or the W key to turn the screen white while you finish what you are saying. Press B or W and then S again to resume the show. If you finish talking before the end of a slide's allocated display time—for example, if you allow time for questions and there are none—you can always click the left mouse button to manually advance to the next slide. (Remember that either of these pacing adjustments will increase or decrease the total length of the presentation.)

Manually advancing an automatic slide show

Taking Care of Logistics

If you will be running your presentation under controlled conditions—in your own office using your own computer, for example, or in a familiar auditorium with equipment you have used before—you can probably skip this section. Otherwise, you should know that Murphy has a field day with electronic slide shows and that sooner or later "anything that can go wrong will go wrong." The only way to thwart Murphy is by preparing adequately.

The first area to take care of is the presentation equipment. Make sure you have everything you need and know how to put it together. Locate the electrical outlets in the room, set up the equipment, and check that everything is working. If someone else is in charge of setup, check in advance that they know exactly what you need, but still make a point of arriving early and, if necessary, turn on the system—just to be sure.

Checking the equipment

Next, check the setup from the point of view of your audience. If you are using a projector, make sure it is the correct distance from the screen and focused to produce the sharpest image. If you are using a microphone, check its volume. Check where the light switches/dimmers are and make sure any lights that can't be dimmed do not shine directly on the screen. Also check that you can sit or stand to the side of the computer table so that you and your audience can see each other but you can also view the screen.

If you are not using your own computer, load your presentation from floppy disk onto the computer's hard drive ahead of time. If possible, rehearse your presentation in the room and with the equipment and lighting you will actually use.

And in case of disaster, duplicate your electronic slide show as a set of overhead transparencies and handouts and bring them with you so that you can switch to this tried-and-true format if necessary. The show must go on!

Emergency accessories

Before you strike off on your own to give an electronic slide show, you should remember to pack a few accessories in case of emergency:

- Checklist of all the items you need for a successful presentation (including such things as speaker's notes and/or handouts, computer cables, mouse pointer, remote control, software and extra disks, and a sound unit/amplifier)
- Overhead transparencies or backup slides
- Small flashlight and extra batteries (so that you can find the keyboard or your notes with the lights dimmed)
- Screwdriver or small wrench (in case you have VGA port connector problems)
- Extension cord (so that you can reach a distant outlet)

Preparing Stand-Alone Presentations

At Online Press, we receive many unsolicited resumés from people looking for work in the training/publishing/computer industries. Recently, we received our first on-line resumé. The job seeker displayed his computer and screen design skills and his initiative and creativity by sending us a PowerPoint presentation that highlighted his qualifications. The disk was accompanied by instructions for loading files onto a hard drive and for running PowerPoint Viewer, which displayed the self-running resumé slide show. In this section, we explore how to create such a stand-alone presentation.

PowerPoint Viewer ————————→ To send a presentation to someone else, you need to copy the presentation file to a disk along with the PowerPoint Viewer program. PowerPoint Viewer is a stripped down version of PowerPoint that displays an electronic slide show in Slide Show view only. Copying PowerPoint Viewer to the disk ensures that recipients can view your presentation whether or not they have PowerPoint on their computers. PowerPoint Viewer comes with PowerPoint and is not subject to the same copyright restrictions as the larger program, so you can copy it as many times as you like. Here's how to set up a disk containing the RECYCLE.PPT presentation:

Copying PowerPoint Viewer to a disk ————→ 1. In your original set of PowerPoint (or Microsoft Office) disks, locate the PowerPoint Viewer disk (disk 11 of the 3 1/2-inch stand-alone PowerPoint disks; disk 31 of the 3 1/2-inch Microsoft Office disks).

2. Switch to File Manager, and choose Copy Disk from the Disk menu to display this dialog box:

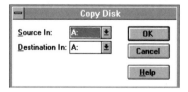

3. If necessary, change the drive letters in the Source In and Destination In edit boxes, and then click OK. When the Confirm Copy Disk message appears, click Yes, insert the source disk in your floppy drive, and click OK. Then, when

requested, insert a blank formatted destination disk in your floppy drive.

4. Put the original PowerPoint Viewer disk away in a safe place with the other original disks, and copy the RECYCLE.PPT file to the disk containing the copy of Viewer. (PowerPoint Viewer's 16 files take up approximately 1.1 MB of space on the disk, so the RECYCLE.PPT presentation will easily fit on the same disk. You might have to copy larger presentation files to their own disk.)

Copying the presentation to the disk

The presentation disk is now ready to send out. To tell the recipient how to view the electronic slide show, you need to send the following instructions with the disk:

Giving instructions

- In File Manager, make a directory called RECYCLE (for our example) in the root directory of the computer's hard drive.

- Copy the contents of the disk to the RECYCLE directory.

- Still in File Manager, choose Run from the File menu, type *c:\recycle\vsetup.exe*, and press Enter. When the Setup dialog box appears, click OK to install PowerPoint Viewer in the C:\PPTVIEW directory. Click OK when setup is complete.

- Locate and double-click the PowerPoint Viewer icon in Program Manager. Then in the Microsoft PowerPoint Viewer dialog box, select RECYCLE.PPT, and click Show.

  If you have set up the presentation to run automatically, tell the recipient to select Use Automatic Timings in the Microsoft PowerPoint Viewer dialog box before clicking Show. If you want the presentation to run continuously, tell the recipient to also select Run Continuously Until Esc.

  If you have set up the presentation to run manually, tell the recipient to click the left mouse button or press PageDown to move to the next slide and click the right mouse button or press PageUp to return to the previous slide.

- When the presentation finishes and PowerPoint Viewer redisplays the Microsoft PowerPoint Viewer dialog box, click Quit to quit PowerPoint Viewer.

Index